D1611859

EDINBURGH UNIVERSITY

WITHDRAWN

30150   008266162

CAMBRIDGE STUDIES
IN ENGLISH LEGAL HISTORY

Edited by
D. E. C. YALE
Fellow of Christ's College
and Reader in English Legal History at the University of Cambridge

MARRIAGE SETTLEMENTS, 1601–1740

THE ADOPTION OF THE STRICT SETTLEMENT

LLOYD BONFIELD

Research Fellow, Trinity College, Cambridge

CAMBRIDGE UNIVERSITY PRESS

CAMBRIDGE

LONDON   NEW YORK   NEW ROCHELLE

MELBOURNE   SYDNEY

EDINBURGH UNIVERSITY LIBRARY

WITHDRAWN

Published by the Press Syndicate of the University of Cambridge
The Pitt Building, Trumpington Street, Cambridge CB2 1RP
32 East 57th Street, New York, NY10022, USA
296 Beaconsfield Parade, Middle Park, Melbourne 3206, Australia

© Cambridge University Press 1983

First published 1983

Printed in Great Britain at the University Press, Cambridge

Library of Congress catalogue card number: 82-19828

British Library Cataloguing in Publication Data

Bonfield, Lloyd
Marriage settlements 1601–1740. – (Cambridge
studies in English legal history)
1. Husband and wife – England
2. Property – England
I. Title
344.2064   KD760
ISBN 0 521 25021 8

To my parents

CONTENTS

TABLES

PREFACE

Doctoral theses often have curious origins. The one which has been revised and is presented here had its genesis in a seminar on the 'Problems of the aristocracy in France and England in the seventeenth and eighteenth centuries' in the University of Iowa when Professors Henry Horwitz and Ralph Giesey found that they had a law student amongst their aspiring historians. It became my task to explain the workings of the strict settlement to my colleagues, and to compare the English system of inheritance with the French. I have lived with this curious device ever since.

It is a pleasure to acknowledge gratefully the kindness which scholars have shown me. Foremost, I should like to thank Professor Sir John Habakkuk who graciously entertained me at the Lodge in Jesus College, Oxford, and unearthed boxes of notes which embodied the research of his seminal works on landownership and marriage settlements. Although I may at times call into question some of his conclusions, all legal and economic historians are indebted to him for his pioneering work on these topics. Mr David Yale supervised the thesis and edited the text for the Cambridge Studies in English Legal History. For his tireless labours, and his friendship, I warmly thank him. Professor Donald Coleman and various members of the Cambridge Group for the History of Population and Social Structure, in particular Dr Peter Laslett, helped me to see the economic and social dimensions of the study. My examiners, Professor Brian Simpson and Dr Christopher Clay, made useful suggestions in the way of revision, as did Dr John Baker who read the entire text with the care and incisiveness that all who know his own work would expect. Professors Richard Helmholz, S. F. C. Milsom and Russell Osgood and Dr Brian Outhwaite read and criticized individual chapters. Any remaining errors are, of course, my own responsibility.

I should like to acknowledge others who supported this project in various ways. Without the financial assistance of the United States –

United Kingdom Educational Association, which brought me to Cambridge as a Fulbright Scholar, and the Master and Fellows of Trinity College, who bestowed upon me the leisure of a research fellowship, this work would have been neither undertaken nor completed. The staff at the County Archives in Kent, Northamptonshire, Staffordshire and Leicestershire graciously met my requests for unreasonably large numbers of family muniments. Dr John Dawson of the Literary and Linguistics Computing Centre saved me countless tedious days of hand sorting the substance of the settlements by developing a method of doing it all by computer. Mrs Mary Pomery cheerfully typed numerous drafts from illegible manuscripts and Ms Susan Green typed the final draft. Finally, I am indebted to my wife, Adriana, for reasons which all who know her will undoubtedly understand.

Cambridge   LLOYD BONFIELD
March, 1982

ABBREVIATIONS

In citing cases, I have employed the standard abbreviation for the appropriate law reports (e.g. Co. Rep., Dyer). Marriage settlements have been cited by computer sequence number instead of the rather cumbersome archives reference. A key which relates sequence numbers to the appropriate archives office reference appears in the bibliography. In addition, the following abbreviations are used in the footnotes:

B.I.H.R.	*Bulletin of the Institute of Historical Research*
B.M.	British Museum
Bl. Comm.	William Blackstone, *Commentaries on the laws of England*, 4th edn (London, 1770)
C.J.	Commons Journals
Co. Litt.	E. Coke, *The first part of the institutes of the laws of England, or a commentary on Littlejohn*, 18th edn, ed. F. Hargrave and C. Butler (London, 1823)
E.H.R.	*English Historical Review*
Econ. Hist. Rev.	*Economic History Review*
H.E.L.	William Holdsworth, *A history of English law* (16 vols., London, 1922–66)
H.M.C.	Historical Manuscripts Commission
K.A.O.	Kent Archives Office
L.R.O.	Leicestershire Record Office
Litt.	*Littleton's tenures in English*, ed. E. Wambaugh (Washington, 1903)
N.R.O.	Northamptonshire Record Office
P.R.O.	Public Record Office
S.P.	State Papers
Simpson, *Land law*	A. W. B. Simpson, *An introduction to the history of the land law* (Oxford, 1961)
T.R.H.S.	*Transactions of the Royal Historical Society*

INTRODUCTION

For the desire of great landowners has constantly been to make the strictest settlements which the law would allow, and the law . . . has set bounds, though liberal ones, to the power of fettering inheritances and suspending absolute ownership. And the ingenuity of conveyancers, devising how to satisfy private ambition within the field left clear to it by public ordinance, has produced that curious and exquisite structure [the strict settlement] which, a hundred years hence, will probably be abandoned to the care of a few legal antiquaries as the learning of disseisin and collateral warranty.

Sir Frederick Pollock,
The Land Laws, 2nd edn (London, 1887), 114–15

In the mid-seventeenth century, conveyancers developed a form of property settlement which was rapidly adopted by most segments of English landed society. With minor modifications this conveyancing precedent, the strict family settlement executed upon the marriage of the eldest son, remained the prevailing means by which landed wealth was transmitted between the generations until the twentieth century when a changing economic and political climate rendered moribund the social structure which the settlement sought to preserve. For more than two centuries, however, much of the land in England was held under strict settlement. Particularly in pre-industrial England, where so vast a proportion of the nation's capital and human resources was invested in land and agricultural production, the restraints which the strict settlement placed upon the freedom of the tenant in possession to alienate, consolidate, or exploit his estate must have had a profound effect upon the economy.

For the most part, however, I shall leave the task of assessing the economic impact of the strict settlement to others; instead, I shall join the ranks of the 'legal antiquaries' where, as Sir Frederick Pollock correctly predicted, this 'curious and exquisite structure' remains of interest. The focus of this monograph will be upon developments in the mechanics of marriage settlements which resulted from the elaboration in the courts of legal doctrine regarding future interests. The prevailing forms of marriage settlement during the period 1601–1740 will be investigated, and in particular, the adoption of the strict settlement in the eighty-odd years after its formulation will be charted.

Such a task requires an incursion into the controversy over perpetuities which raged in the courts of common law and equity during the late sixteenth and early seventeenth centuries. In the main, legal historians have categorized the period as one of great uncertainty in the land law. It will be suggested, however, that several threads of legal doctrine were established during this period which enabled conveyancers to effect the intergenerational transfer of the patrimony by marriage settlement. Essentially, the development of legal theory to conveyancing practice will be related and the similarity between the prevailing form of marriage settlement in the early seventeenth century and the strict settlement will be illustrated. Once this initial mode of settlement had been established, a life estate in the tenant in possession followed by an entail in his unborn eldest son, conveyancers set out to protect the contingent entail in the unborn son, and the strict settlement was spawned.

At times, however, I shall be treading upon the territory of economic historians since my concern lies also with the ramifications of the trends in marriage settlements. In particular, two points will be addressed. First, the proffered connection between the strict settlement and the 'rise of great estates' in the period 1680–1740 will be assessed.[1] Secondly, the changing pattern of provisions for younger sons and daughters by marriage settlement will be traced in an attempt to determine whether the strict settlement was, as Sir William Blackstone suggested, developed to secure provisions for the children of the impending marriage.[2] Thus I shall be enmeshed in the controversy over the workings of marriage and inheritance in the late seventeenth and early eighteenth centuries, but squarely within the context of the strict settlement. How the trends in settlement practice will be established is central to the validity and the strength of the conclusions, and it is therefore necessary to explain, and to defend, the methodology employed.

In commenting upon empirical research in the social sciences, Professor Arthur Schlesinger Jr noted that 'almost all important

1 H. J. Habakkuk, 'English landownership 1680–1740', *Econ. Hist. Rev.*, X (1940).
2 2 *Bl. Comm.*, 172.

[historical] questions are important precisely because they are *not* susceptible to quantitative answers'.[3] It is not my intention here to debate the merits of quantification in history; others have taken up the challenge.[4] However, in attempting to resolve historical questions, important or otherwise, it is incumbent upon the historian to exploit the available evidence in the most propitious manner. In attempting to illuminate conveyancing *practice*, as opposed to *theory*, it seemed appropriate to study as large a quantity of settlements as possible, and to exploit mechanical aids where they could be of assistance. Thus instead of embarking upon a study of a family or group of families whose settlements have been preserved, I resolved to select two counties and examine *all* of the settlements executed during the period which have been preserved in the county archives.

I am, however, aware of the limitations of this method of establishing the developments in marriage settlements. Although I have studied over 230 settlements executed during the period 1601–1740, this group constitutes a small percentage of the total number of marriage settlements executed by the peerage and gentry. Moreover, I realize that my group of settlements may well be biased; the mere fact that these settlements survive while the majority have been lost does not render the group a 'random sample'. Indeed, by virtue of their survival these settlements are by definition 'atypical'. But in many areas of the discipline, historians do not operate in a quantitative paradise. Given the nature of the evidence, I believe that my approach is the one *most* calculated to resolve the questions which I have set out to determine. In stating my conclusions, however, the researcher, and the reader, must recognize the limitations of the data set.

To determine the extent of the marriage settlements which survive was a time-consuming and somewhat monotonous task. It was necessary to sift through numerous catalogues of title deeds to extract the marriage settlements. Once the body of surviving settlements was ascertained, the various clauses had to be sorted to establish the patterns of legal form and disposition. With technical

3 Arthur Schlesinger Jr, 'The humanist looks at empirical social research', *American Sociological Review*, 27 (1962), 770; quoted in W. O. Aydelotte, *Quantification in history* (Reading, Mass., 1971), 55.
4 In particular see the essays of Professor Aydelotte in *Quantification*; and the Introduction to R. Floud, *An introduction to quantitative methods for historians* (London, 1973).

assistance,[5] a method was developed to sort the clauses by computer. This process aided immeasurably in establishing the patterns of settlement which will be illustrated in the succeeding chapters. Finally, in defining the limitations of my data set, something must be said about the peculiarities of the counties under study. First let us consider Kent. During the seventeenth and early eighteenth centuries, Kent was a county with an exceptionally large body of gentry. Yet the actual numbers remain uncertain. Contemporary and modern estimates vary greatly, and these judgments are largely educated guesses.[6] Moreover, the origins of the gentry, a factor which may well have influenced their settlement habits, are also in dispute. Professor Coleman[7] reckons that the appraisal of William Lambarde in the sixteenth century holds true for the mid-seventeenth and early eighteenth century as well: 'The Gentlemen be not here (throughout) of so ancient stocks as else where, especially in the parts neere to London, from which citie (as it were from a certaine rich and wealthy seedplot) Courtiers, Lawyers, and Merchants be continually translated.'[8] Professor Everitt, however, considers the gentry for the most part to be indigenous.[9]

5 I am indebted to Dr John Dawson of the University of Cambridge Literary and Linguistics Computing Centre for his assistance in developing a method to code the rather cumbersome clauses of the settlements.
6 Professor Everitt estimates the body of gentry to be 'at least 800 and possibly more than 1,000'. No contemporary source which he cites estimated such a large number. A. M. Everitt, *The community of Kent and the Great Rebellion* (Leicester, 1973), 33–4. Cf. T. P. R. Laslett, 'The gentry of Kent in 1640', *Cambridge Historical Journal*, X (1949).
7 D. C. Coleman, 'The economy of Kent under the later Stuarts' (Unpublished University of London Ph.D. thesis, 1951), part III. Cf. D. C. Coleman, *Sir John Banks: baronet and businessman* (Oxford, 1963), 97.
8 William Lambarde, *A perambulation of Kent* (London, 1596), 12–13.
9 Everitt, *Community of Kent*, 37. Cf. A. M. Everitt, 'Kent and its gentry, 1640–60, a political study' (Unpublished University of London Ph.D. thesis, 1957), Appendix IV. My rather unsophisticated contribution to the controversy tends to confirm Professor Coleman's view. By tracing the descent of manors in Edward Hasted, *The history and topographical survey of the county of Kent* (4 vols., Canterbury, 1778–99), the mean number of 'turnovers' of manors during the period 1601–1720 was 2.07. Thus the 'average' manor saw a new owner about every 40 years. Admittedly, there appears to have been a core of indigenous and stable families, but they controlled a rather insubstantial proportion of the manors. I should also state that in my 'counting of manors', I considered the unit as one rendering a degree of social rather than economic status. As Professor Coleman has demonstrated, the value of a manor in economic terms was often

A final peculiarity of Kent, the custom of gavelkind, is worthy of note. Although slowly losing favour amongst the upper reaches of landed society, the tradition of partible inheritances may have rendered Kentish families more inclined to endow their younger sons. In assessing the effects of gavelkind upon landownership, however, it must be recalled that partibility occurred only in instances of intestate succession; a landowner who wished to strengthen his patriline at the expense of his younger sons could circumvent the operation of gavelkind by executing a settlement or will.[10]

In some respects, though, Kent is an ideal county to consider. While some may consider Kent to be a 'home county', and therefore more susceptible to the influence of innovations from London, Professor Everitt has noted that geography renders parts of Kent decidedly remote; Canterbury is in fact further from London than is Cambridge.[11] Thus landed society in Kent was composed of a mixture of indigenous gentry and newcomers, cosmopolitan to some extent, yet partially insular.

In selecting a county for the purposes of comparison, geography appeared to be the most salient consideration. It seemed most appropriate to choose a county in the Midlands; and Northamptonshire was selected for two reasons. The first was practical: the county archives in Northampton contained the largest number of settlements. Secondly, Northamptonshire is the county where the proffered 'rise of great estates' occurred. Treading upon Professor Habakkuk's terrain would therefore be useful in testing the nexus between the strict settlement and 'the rise of great estates'.

In addition, the two counties provide a contrast owing to the supposed origins of the gentry. Professor Everitt has argued that unlike their Kentish counterparts the Northamptonshire gentry were of much more recent origin.[12] Such a difference might account for contrasts in settlement practice. While a comparative study of two counties does not permit broad generalizations for the whole of

negligible: Coleman, 'Economy of Kent', 35. For a contrary view, see C. W. Chalkin, *Seventeenth century Kent* (London, 1965), 54, and Peter Clark, *English provincial society from the Reformation to the Revolution* (Sussex, 1977), 397.
10 *Co. Litt.*, 11b. Cf. Thomas Robinson, *The common law of Kent: or the customs of gavelkind* (London, 1788), Chapter V.
11 Everitt, *Community of Kent*, 22.
12 A. M. Everitt, 'Social mobility in early modern England', *Past and Present*, XXX (1966), 64.

England, the differences between the two counties enlarge the scope for possible conclusions. Constraints of time dictate certain limits to the areas which can be examined in detail.

To conclude this introduction, I should like to re-affirm the interdisciplinary nature of this study. I believe that it is appropriate to view the law touching settlements in historical perspective as both a legal and an economic phenomenon; by determining the extent to which one could control the disposition of the patrimony in a society in which land was the chief source of wealth, the judges were exercising a rudimentary form of 'trade regulation'. The opinions of the judges suggest that they were aware of the economic ramifications of their decisions; and modern legal historians should share that awareness. This monograph is a modest attempt to enlighten them.

1

THE MEDIEVAL INHERITANCE AND THE
STATUTE OF USES

The making of financial arrangements at marriage has been a concern of landed families in England since Anglo-Saxon times. In a society with high mortality and one in which men controlled the bulk of wealth-producing property, perhaps the most pressing concern was to secure provision for women who survived their husbands. The Anglo-Saxons provided for their widows through the institution of *morgengifu*.[1] Early on, the common law recognized the obligation of the groom to endow his wife at the church door, and directed an appropriation of land at his death if he failed to do so.[2] Towards the close of the Middle Ages the provision for maintenance was coupled with the transmission of the patrimony between the generations by marriage settlement.[3] The early modern marriage settlement, the subject of this study, was an elaboration of this medieval form.

The increased incidence of marriage settlements in the fourteenth century can in part be attributed to the popularity of feoffments to uses. Because common law dower attached only to lands of which her husband had stood seised, a widow could not claim her thirds in land held to his use. Legal commentators in the sixteenth century who opposed uses argued that one of their most serious consequences was that they deprived widows of their

1 Ernest Young, 'The Anglo-Saxon family law', in *Essays in Anglo-Saxon law* (Boston, Mass., 1905), 174. Young suggested linear development in provisions for widows from the *morgengifu* through to the forms of dower recognized by Littleton.
2 F. Pollock and F. W. Maitland, *The history of English law before the time of Edward I*, 2nd edn (2 vols., Cambridge, 1968), II, 420–8; *The treatise on the laws and customs of the realm of England commonly called Glanvill*, ed. G. D. G. Hall (London, 1965), Book VI, 1; *Bracton on the laws and customs of England*, ed. S. E. Thorne (4 vols., Cambridge, Mass., 1968–), II, 265–8.
3 J. M. W. Bean, *The decline of English feudalism, 1215–1540* (Manchester, 1968), 114–28; Simpson, *Land law*, 218.

1

dower.[4] Modern historians, however, have a more balanced view, citing examples of directions to feoffees which allow land in excess of the third permitted at common law.[5] Regardless, if a substantial proportion of a landowner's estate was held in use it was necessary to execute a settlement which specified maintenance for the bride if she survived the groom. Normally the bride and groom were granted a joint life estate, or jointure as it was called, with a remainder in tail to their heirs male.[6] Consequently the woman would hold the specified estates to her own use for her life if she survived her husband, and upon her death they would pass to the eldest son. In this manner, feoffment to uses came to deal with the two major concerns of the early modern marriage settlement: the fixing of maintenance should the bride survive her husband and the hereditary transmission of the patrimony.

Since marriage settlements were effected by feoffments to uses it has been suggested that the enactment of the Statute of Uses[7] in 1536 significantly altered the means by which landowners settled their estates.[8] A more detailed enquiry of early-sixteenth-century settlements must be undertaken to confirm this hypothesis, but the transformation of hitherto equitable estates into legal interests which the statute engendered did affect the position of widows. Dower could be claimed in estates held by way of use which the statute had transformed into a legal interest.

In families where jointures had been executed by settlement, therefore, the widow might have been able by virtue of the statute to enjoy her jointure lands and also claim common law dower. This unwanted consequence of the operation of the statute was prevented by certain provisions embodied in the Act; specifically,

4 For example, Bacon's 'Reading upon the Statute of Uses', in *Works of Lord Bacon*, ed. J. Spedding (London, 1857), VII, 418; *St German's Doctor and Student*, ed. T. F. T. Plucknett and J. Barton (Seldon Society, London, 1974), 91, 224: 'The evil consequence of uses', reprinted in *H.E.L.*, IV, 577–80, no. 16.
5 Bean, *Decline of English feudalism*, 136–7; M. E. Avery, 'The history of equitable jurisdiction of Chancery before 1460', *B.I.H.R.*, XLII (1969), 139–44.
6 G. A. Holmes, *The estates of the higher nobility in fourteenth century England* (Cambridge, 1957), 41–5; K. B. McFarlane, *The nobility of later medieval England* (Oxford, 1973), 64–7, 85–6; J. P. Cooper, 'Patterns of inheritance and settlement by great landowners from the fifteenth to the eighteenth centuries', in *Family and inheritance*, ed. J. Goody, J. Thirsk and E. P. Thompson (Cambridge, 1976), 200–1.
7 27 Hen. VIII c. 10.
8 Cooper, 'Patterns of inheritance', 203.

section 6 stipulated that the widow could not have both her jointure and her dower. With respect to pre-existing and future marriage agreements, widows who agreed to jointure were precluded from claiming their dower.

But the statute went further; and a subsequent provision had a considerable effect upon the future pattern of settlement.[9] The statute provided that those widows who had accepted jointures prior to marriage were barred from renouncing the allocation and claiming their dower at common law. However, the same was not the case with regard to post-nuptial agreements; here the widow was free to renounce her jointure 'and take her dower by a writ of dower or otherwise according to the Common law'. The effect of the statute, therefore, was to press those landowners who wished to fix immutably the bride's jointure to execute a settlement prior to marriage. Because the consent of the bride's family was necessary, considerable leverage was bestowed upon them with respect to the disposition of the groom's patrimony embodied in the settlement. The ability to make jointures was so crucial to effect a suitable marriage that it was often read into pre-existing settlements:

And it is great reason, although he willed that the order of his inheritance should be preserved, yet to make a provision for jointure; and it is a great reason and cause to his family to enable and make them capable of great matches, which should be a strengthening to his posterity, which could not be without great jointures, wherefore I conceive it reasonable to construe it so, that here they have power to make jointures for their wives.[10]

One of the effects of the Statute of Uses, then, was that it encouraged the execution of pre-nuptial marriage settlements which contained provisions both for jointure and for the transmission of the estate between the generations.

During the sixteenth century, a body of law concerning the appropriate mechanics for creating a jointure was fashioned. Coke noted that 'to the making of a perfect joynture within that statute six things are to be observed'.[11] The first requirement was that the jointure estate must take effect 'presently after the decease of her husband'.[12] To constitute a binding jointure, it was necessary for the wife to come into enjoyment of her interest immediately upon

9 The eighth section.
10 *Read* v. *Nash* (1589), 1 Leon. 147, 147–8.
11 *Co. Litt.*, 36b.
12 *Ibid.*

the death of her husband. The most effective method of meeting this requirement was for the settlement to grant a joint life estate to the prospective husband and wife, or else limit successive life estates to their use.[13] As Coke noted, the limitation of an intervening estate to a stranger after the husband's death, perhaps to his executor, followed by an estate limited to the wife did not create a valid jointure. On the other hand, a jointure could be raised even though the estate was upon condition.[14]

The second requirement dealt with the quality of estate which was to comprise the jointure. According to the statute, it was necessary for the assurance to be to the wife 'for the term of her life or otherwise in jointure'.[15] Initially there was some controversy over the interpretation of the word 'otherwise'. In *Dame Dennis' Case*,[16] a marriage settlement had been executed which granted a fee simple to the husband and wife, and there was a diversity of opinion as to whether such an interest could constitute a valid jointure. Catlyn, Saunders, and Dyer preferred a broader construction, and argued that limitations in fee simple were within the equity of the statute. Browne and Whyddon cited authority from the reign of Edward VI reported by Brooke which allowed only life estates and estates in fee tail. From the report of the case by Dyer, it would appear that the latter view prevailed. Coke's report in *Vernon's Case*,[17] however, suggests that it was agreed by 1572 that Brooke had misreported the case. Nevertheless, by this time it was clear that limitations in fee simple could constitute a valid jointure. It was, however, agreed that as a third requirement the estate had to be granted to the wife herself; an estate limited to others in trust for the wife was insufficient.[18]

The final requirements noted by Coke dealt with the mechanics of creating the jointure estate. In the first place it was essential that the jointure be in total and not partial satisfaction of dower. Although no specific language within the act directed such a rule, it was likely thought that the intent of the statute was for dower and jointure to be mutually exclusive. Such an interpretation must have

13 *Villers* v. *Beamon* (1557), Dyer 146a, 148a.
14 *Vernon's Case* (1572), 4 Co. Rep. 1.
15 The sixth section.
16 (1572), Dyer 248a.
17 4 Co. Rep. 1.
18 *Co. Litt.*, 36b.

seemed obvious, at least to Coke, who considered that the requirement 'is so plaine as it needeth not any example'.[19]
    Coke's fifth requirement was that the instrument had to aver that
the jointure was created in satisfaction of dower. This was based
upon the words of the statute: that the interest was to be 'in manner
or form expressed . . . for the jointure of the wife'.[20] But this
requirement was not adhered to strictly. In *Ashton's Case*,[21] for
example, a feoffment was made to the bride for her life prior to her
marriage in pursuance of 'certain covenants contained in a pair of
indentures . . . concerning a marriage'. Although the feoffment did
not express that the estate was in jointure in satisfaction of dower, it
was held to create a valid jointure. Perhaps the court was influenced
by the existence of the original agreement, because three years later
in an anonymous case[22] the judges were less lenient. A widow had
taken possession of lands pursuant to a post-nuptial settlement and
then had sued for her dower; Dyer noted: 'Whether this matter
generally alleged without averment that it was for jointure or dower
shall be a bar to dower or not, *quaere* well, for the words of the statute
of 27 [Henry VIII] are expressly for the jointure of the wife.'[23] It
was not until the late seventeenth century that the word 'jointure'
alone was held sufficient.[24]
    The final requirement was that a jointure had to be made either
before an intended or after an existing marriage.[25] For the jointure
to be binding, however, the statute stipulated that the agreement be
executed prior to marriage. It is unclear as to why the widow was
allowed to renounce a jointure executed after marriage even though
she consented to the agreement. Perhaps it was thought that wives
might be compelled by their husbands to accept the jointures. Such
an argument might be more persuasive if the woman's consent was
necessary in arranging jointure by a pre-nuptial settlement. But this
was not the case, since parental consent was sufficient to bind the
bride. Because of the *feme covert*'s general inability to contract, the

19 *Ibid.*
20 The sixth section.
21 (1565), Dyer 228a.
22 (1568), Dyer 266a.
23 *Ibid.*
24 Or so Lord Chancellor Somers held in *Lawrence* v. *Lawrence* (1699), 2 Vern. 365.
    Lord Keeper Wright reversed the decree in 1702, but Somers's position
    eventually prevailed in an unreported case: *Vizard* v. *Longdale* cited by Lord
    Hardwicke in *Walker* v. *Walker* (1747), 1 Ves. Sen. 55.
25 *Co. Litt.*, 36b. This is perhaps a somewhat obvious requirement.

non-binding nature of a post-nuptial settlement would appear consistent with her legal position.

In the course of the sixteenth century, the settling of jointure was becoming increasingly popular.[26] Commentators noted its practical advantages over dower.[27] In the first place, since a jointure created prior to marriage barred dower claims, the husband was free to deal with the residue of the patrimony as he pleased, particularly with regard to alienations. It was only with respect to the jointure lands that the consent of the widow was necessary in order to alienate. Where a jointure had been created, the purchaser could be certain that the lands which he bought were free of dower claims. Moreover, there were considerable advantages to the prospective heir in effecting a settlement which barred dower. To him, such claims were often a nuisance, preventing him from consolidating his estate and interfering with his freedom of alienation.[28] Because a jointure specified the lands which the widow was to enjoy, these two problems were avoided, as well as the often arduous task of sorting out a common law dower. There were advantages to the bride in jointure as well; upon marriage, she became seised of an immediate estate of inheritance, and upon her husband's death she could enter without suing out a writ. Moreover, her consent was necessary for her husband to alienate jointure land.

The increased incidence of marriage settlements after the Statute of Uses may therefore be ascribed at least in part to the desire of both families to fix jointures, and we may now consider their form in more detail. Unlike their Anglo-Saxon counterparts,[29] medieval marriage settlements often directed the hereditary transmission of the patrimony. The avoidance of feudal dues may have prompted some settlors to employ the settlements to this end but after the statute, and the enactment of the Statute of Wills, other reasons must have prompted settlors.[30] Perhaps the most significant

---

26 M. L. Cioni, 'Women and law in Elizabethan England with particular reference to the Court of Chancery' (Unpublished University of Cambridge Ph.D. thesis, 1974), 198.

27 *Co. Litt.*, 36b; *The lawes resolution of women's rights* (London, 1632), 182–3.

28 I address this question in more detail elsewhere: L. Bonfield, 'Marriage settlements 1660–1740: The adoption of the strict settlement in Kent and Northamptonshire', in *Marriage and society*, ed. R. B. Outhwaite (London, 1981), 101–15.

29 A. J. Robertson, *Anglo-Saxon charters* (Cambridge, 1939), LXXVI, LXXVII.

30 J. L. Barton has recently stressed the financial advantages of such a settlement where the entail was limited to the settlor's grandson: J. L. Barton, 'Future

was to effect the orderly transmission of the patrimony in the manner which the landowner desired. The alternative to the settlement was the will, but it was less satisfactory. Wills were often executed on one's deathbed, without the assistance of a lawyer.[31] Enumerating all the various parcels of land which comprised the patrimony would have been awkward. Without the assistance of counsel a complex disposition would not be possible. Then, as now, the deathbed was not the most appropriate place for prudent estate planning. Moreover, sloppy draftsmanship might pave the way to an expensive lawsuit regarding matters of interpretation.

Thus the early modern marriage settlement accomplished two goals: immutably fixing the bride's jointure and transmitting the patrimony between the generations in the manner desired by the landowner. The forms which these dispositions assumed are of great interest to the legal historian, and are the concern of this monograph. In the succeeding chapter, it will be suggested that the period after the Statute of Uses witnessed the emergence of two types of settlement, one which secured the orderly transmission of the patrimony and the other which attempted to go further: to deprive succeeding generations of freedom of disposition. The validity of particular settlement forms, and consequently the ability to attain specific 'estate planning' goals, was determined by the courts during the sixteenth and early seventeenth centuries, a period considered one of great uncertainty in the land law. A system of jurisprudence which sanctions innovation retrospectively, that is only when forms of settlement are controverted, necessarily breeds some degree of turmoil. The extent of the uncertainty, however, depends upon the amount of experimentation, and whether secure alternative forms exist. During our period, cautious landowners always had the option of executing settlements whose validity had been accepted by the judges.

interests and royal revenues in the sixteenth century', in *On the laws and customs of England: essays in honor of Samuel E. Thorne*, ed. M. S. Arnold, T. A. Green, S. A. Scully and S. D. White (Chapel Hill, North Carolina, 1981), 321.

31 Henry Swinburne suggested that only the 'ruder and more ignorant people' were reluctant to make wills whilst in good health fearing that so doing would have an adverse effect upon their life expectancy. But his discussion of written testaments suggests that deathbed dispositions were not unknown amongst the better sort. Henry Swinburne, *A briefe treatise of testaments and last wills* (London, 1635), 43, 39–40. See also J. March, *Amicus republicae: the commonwealth's friend* (London, 1651), 157–8; and Pollock and Maitland, *History of English law*, II, 314, 337, 356.

Eventually, settlements which unduly attempted to circumscribe freedom of alienation, perpetuities and the like, were disallowed. But the common law courts in the late sixteenth and early seventeenth centuries ultimately sanctioned a less restrictive form, one in which a life estate was limited to a living person with an entail in remainder granted to his unborn heir. This concession was significant because it allowed for the transmission of the patrimony by marriage settlement, while conferring some protection against alienation by the tenant in possession. It was from this form that the strict settlement was developed.

But to argue that it was experimentation followed by judicial sanction which led to the widespread adoption of a particular form of settlement requires one to ascertain what came before. Unfortunately, it is far more difficult to establish practice before the turn of the seventeenth century given the dearth of surviving settlements amongst family muniments. There is, however, a less satisfactory source, but one which accurately details the forms of settlement: the law reports. Embodied within the printed cases are numerous actions involving settlements. In many of the cases the form of settlement is not controverted so a data set based upon this evidence is not biased towards settlements of dubious validity.

In order to gain an impression of sixteenth-century settlement forms, and it must be admitted that the evidence employed permits no more than this, I have extracted the settlements noted in the reports of Plowden, Dyer, Leonard, Coke, and Croke. All settlements have been included in order to construct a larger body of data. It would appear to be legitimate to make no distinction between marriage and family settlements since during the period they do not differ in legal mechanics. Two distinct forms emerge, and their frequency is tabulated in Table 1. During the sixteenth century, the most common form of settlement was the limitation of an entail to a living person or persons; in marriage settlements the entail was granted to the prospective groom and bride, and in family settlements to the male heir. The actual wording of the grant was: 'to groom and bride and the heirs male of their two bodies begotten'. During the reign of Elizabeth, an alternative form appears with reasonable frequency: the 'life estate-entail' mode. In this disposition, a successive life estate or a joint life estate was limited to the groom and bride with the entail secured in the male heir produced by the marriage. Although this form of settlement was not novel – examples appear in the reign of Henry VIII[32] – the life estate-entail mode would seem to be exceptional until the latter part of the reign of Elizabeth. Conveyancing books, both printed and manuscript, appear to confirm this trend.[33]

Table 1 *Sixteenth-century settlement practice* (N = 172)

Settlement forms	Pre-Statute of Uses N	%	1536– 1558 N	%	Eliza- bethan N	%	Unknown N	%	Totals N	%
Entail to living person	26	96.3	29	90.6	34	82.9	66	91.6	155	90.1
Life estate-entail	–	–	1	3.1	6	14.6	3	4.2	10	5.8
Other forms	1	3.7	2	6.3	1	2.4	3	4.2	7	4.1
Totals	27	100.0	32	100.0	41	99.9	72	100.0	172	100.0

The settlements under consideration highlight two points. The first is that the Statute of Uses had little impact upon the legal form employed in marriage settlements. What it may have done was to encourage the execution of pre-nuptial settlements to fix jointures. These settlements, like their medieval predecessors, also directed the hereditary disposition of the patrimony. Secondly, it would appear that there was considerable uniformity in settlement practice, and that male heirs were destined to come into possession of their estates as tenants in tail with powers of deposition.

To conclude, then, the provision of maintenance for widows at marriage has long been a concern of English landowners. Common law dower initially limited the quantity of land which could comprise the widow's maintenance to a third of her husband's

32 Examples of 'life estate-entail' settlements can be found in decisions noted in *Spelman's reports*, ed. J. H. Baker (Selden Society, London, 1977), 93, 210, 226; but the majority of settlements in the reports confer entails as discussed above; 225, 226, 228.

33 The first printed conveyancing book to contain examples of 'life estate-entail' settlements is W. West's *Symbolaeographia* (London, 1590), 25–7. Thomas Phaer printed a marriage settlement which granted an entail to the bride and groom, *A newe boke of presidents in manner of a register* (London, 1543), lxiii. No marriage settlement of the period is printed in Thomas Madox, *Formulare anglicanum* (London, 1702). For 'life estate-entail' settlements in Elizabethan manuscript precedent notebooks, see B.L., Add. MS 29871, fos. 30–1, 32, 54–5, 70–1; B.L., Add. MS 25240, fos. 24–5, 31–3, 37–8, 139–40, 144–6; C.U.L. MS Ee. iv. 1, fos. 185–7.

estates. With the introduction of feoffments to uses, individual discretion and negotiation determined the amount of provision. By the time of Littleton, the common law of dower had become more flexible, allowing a groom to endow his wife with as much of his estate as he deemed prudent. But the institution of uses in the fourteenth century had a considerable impact upon the financial arrangements at marriage, because the determination of maintenance for the widow was combined with the decision regarding the devolution of the patrimony. The complex marriage settlements of the early modern period are descended from these medieval conveyances. While the Statute of Uses had little impact upon the legal mechanics employed in the dispositions, it did tend to encourage their execution prior to marriage. It was not until the latter part of the sixteenth century that experimentation with regard to mechanics began to occur, and it is to those developments that we may now turn.

2

LAW IN TRANSITION: THE CONFLICT OVER RESTRAINTS UPON ALIENATION

It is commonplace to consider the century and a quarter between the enactment of the Statute of Uses[1] and the development of the strict settlement as an era of great uncertainty in the land law. Legal historians have cited the succession of cases which invalidated various clauses in settlements and wills, as well as the comments of distinguished members of the bar, to attest to this sense of profound confusion.[2] Indeed, Sir Francis Bacon's oft-quoted statement in his argument in *Chudleigh's Case*[3] may well summarize the verdict of modern historians: 'It is likely that Counsellors of the law have advised men in such cases [regarding settlements] that when the cases come to be scanned it is hard to argue how the law will be taken.'[4] Yet his statement must be read in context, as the argument of counsel; no doubt Bacon's modern brethren often express such reservations to their clients, and have been known to echo similar sentiments in court to bolster their arguments.

The purpose of this chapter is to consider the state of the law regarding the settlement of land in the sixteenth and early seventeenth centuries in order to ascertain the extent of uncertainty and its implications for settlement practice. While it must be conceded that few are the periods in which the common law remained static, neither contemporaries nor modern legal historians have ever effectively demonstrated the extent to which this uncertainty affected the fortunes of the landowning class. An examination of the relevant cases suggests that all was not unsettled, but that much of the law was in transition.[5] In particular, two

1 27 Hen. VIII c. 10.
2 See generally, *H.E.L*, VII, 92, 118; and Simpson, *Land law*, chapter IX.
3 (1595), 1 Co. Rep. 120a.
4 Bacon, *Works*, VII, 623.
5 When the arguments in the chapter were first formulated, I did not have the benefit of Mr Barton's essay, 'Future interests and royal revenue'. Although our focus is upon different aspects of the issue of restraints upon alienation, it would appear that our views are not broadly inconsistent.

11

separate, though interrelated, developments were under way during the period following the enactment of the Statute of Uses. First, the courts were considering and defining the manner in which future interests, both legal and equitable, could be manipulated to effect settlements; and secondly, the judges were grappling with the problem of restraints upon alienation. Clearly the failure of the courts to perceive the problem of long-term settlements, the point of interrelation, in terms of remoteness of vesting, and their persistence in basing decisions upon technicality of form did create a body of complex law.

However, as students of the history of the law of real property can painfully attest, complexity had long been a feature of the land law. It is therefore imperative at the outset of an enquiry into developments in the law regarding settlements to appreciate the distinction between a highly technical but rational body of law which, regardless of how confusing it may appear to laymen, can be utilized by practitioners to draft secure settlements, and case law which is in a state of flux. Admittedly the indecision of the common law courts in determining the impact of the Statute of Uses upon executory interests fostered a measure of uncertainty in the law touching future interests. Yet, with regard to the operation of contingent remainders, some decisions actually rendered certain forms of disposition more secure while also allowing for a modicum of flexibility in the execution of marriage settlements. Where uncertainty arose was in the determination of the outer limits of control which could be effected by the manipulation of legal and equitable future interests. Concerning contingent remainders, the focus turned to the relative uncertainty of the contingency occurring. However, the test developed, one of 'possibilities' proved to be unsuitable because there were far too many contingencies which settlors might devise; and the distinction between those which were too remote, and therefore unacceptable, and those which were not too remote was far too hazy to provide a useful guide to settlors. With regard to executory interests, the courts sanctioned the manipulation of uses to create settlements with longer-term effects until *Chudleigh's Case*, where the opinion suggested that the rules of destructibility of contingent remainders ought also to apply to contingent uses. While the legal niceties developed by the common lawyers highlighted in the case law regarding the manipulation of future interests have captured the interest of legal historians, it was

precisely the points of certainty with regard to contingent remainders which allowed for the development of the strict
settlement.

Thus it has been suggested by Professor Habakkuk that 'we
should regard the emergence of the fully fledged strict settlement as
the result not merely of a specific emergency like the civil war but of
a long process of experiment by conveyancers in search of a method
by which landed families could keep their estates intact'.[6] In terms of
legal mechanics, however, this evolution has not yet been illuminated. In this chapter, developments in the law regarding the
employment of future interests in *inter vivos* and testamentary
settlements will be investigated; and in the following chapter a
connection will be established between alterations in the law
regarding these interests and the emergence of a new mode of land
settlement from which the strict settlement was developed.

Such a task requires an incursion into the development of the law
regarding future interests, and the struggle of the common law
courts with the thorny problem of restraints upon alienation. Before
embarking upon a survey of the land law in the sixteenth and early
seventeenth centuries, two points concerning restraints upon
alienation[7] need to be made by way of preface. First, it should be
recognized that despite some periods of vacillation, the common
law has generally been opposed to them.[8] After the acceptance of the
common recovery as a means to bar entails,[9] however, long-term
restraints upon alienation were generally accomplished by employing equitable estates which were beyond the purview of the

---

6 M. E. Finch, *Five Northamptonshire families* (Northamptonshire Record Society,
   Oxford, 1956), Introduction by H. J. Habakkuk, xv.
7 In this chapter, the word 'perpetuity' will not be used in its modern sense, as an
   invalid restraint upon alienation. Sixteenth- and seventeenth-century lawyers
   considered a perpetuity to be a particular form of restraint upon alienation in
   which the right to beneficial enjoyment of an estate was forfeited upon an attempt
   to alienate. For example, note the definition in *The use of the law* (London, 1629),
   58; and that of William Sheppard in *A grand abridgement of the common and statute
   law of England* (3 vols., London, 1675), III, 17. For the sake of clarity, I shall use
   the term in its contemporary sense only, and the words 'lengthy settlement' or the
   like to denote a 'modern perpetuity'.
8 *Bl. Comm.*, 116–19; *H.E.L.*, VII, 193; and Simpson *Land law*, 195.
9 Tradition has it that the common recovery was first sanctioned in *Taltarum's Case*,
   Y.B. 12 Edw. IV, Mich., 15, pl. 16; Prof. Simpson (*Land law*, 173) argues that it
   does not emerge in 'Its fully developed form' until the reign of Henry VIII. Dr
   John Baker in his Introduction to *Spelman's reports* (Selden Society, London,
   1978), 94, 204, believes it was in regular use before 1472.

common law courts. After the enactment of the Statute of Uses, the common law courts began to consider the validity of settlements by way of use.[10] Although initially the courts accepted the flexibility of the use, the decision in *Chudleigh's Case*[11] reversed this trend. Wavering upon this issue came only after 1609 in the common law court's treatment of executory devises of terms.[12] However, the judges were not unmindful that these future interests might be manipulated to create perpetuities; indeed they were not reluctant to express their reservation in these opinions. Moreover, contemporary juristic opinion was generally opposed to restraints upon alienation.[13] Those settlors dabbling with perpetuities were thus forewarned much earlier than 1614[14] that restraints upon alienation were in disfavour even though precedents could be cited in their support.[15]

Secondly, it should be noted that perpetuities were not a sixteenth-century innovation, and that the extent of their employment in family settlements has never been adequately documented.[16] In a recent study of the settlement patterns of the 'great landowners', J. P. Cooper argued that perpetuities were commonly employed in both settlements and wills in the fifteenth century.[17] Nevertheless, he concluded that the incidence of such restraints increased after 1560, even though they often engendered con-

---

10 The common law courts heard cases upon uses prior to the enactment of the statute. But these cases dealt with the statute 1 Rich. III c. 1 which made the conveyances of the *cestue que use* binding, and not with consideration of the quality of the equitable interest. S. F. C. Milsom, *Historical foundations of the common law*, 2nd edn (London, 1981), 214–16.

11 (1595), 1 Co. Rep. 113b.

12 *Manning's Case* (1609), 8 Co. Rep. 94b; *Lampet's Case* (1612), 10 Co. Rep. 46b.

13 See below, pp. 15–24.

14 The date of *Mary Portington's Case* (1614), 10 Co. Rep. 35b, where the Court of Common Pleas held as a matter of policy that any attempt to create an unbarrable entail would fail.

15 In particular, *Scholastica's Case* (1572), Plowden 408; and *Rudhull v. Milwards* (1586), Moo. K.B. 212.

16 The remarks of contemporaries regarding the types of settlement employed should not be accepted without question. It may be instructive to note that in his exposition upon the Statute of Uses, Bacon ventured the opinion that elaborate settlements with remainders to unborn persons did not precede the Statute of Uses. Bacon, *Works*, VII, 409. This view is accepted by J. Williams, 'On the origins of the present mode of family settlements of landed property', *Papers read before the Juridical Society*, I (1855–8). But note *Manning and Andrew's Case* (1576), 1 Leon. 356, where the settlement was drafted in 1517; and cf. Cooper, 'Patterns of inheritance', Appendix I.

17 Cooper, 'Patterns of inheritance', 204.

troversy between the heir male and the heir general. However, Mr Cooper limited his discussion of inheritance customs to the peers, who by his own calculations controlled only one-half of the holdings of the greater landowners.[18] Thus we remain ignorant of the settlement practices of the gentry, who controlled the greatest portion of the landed wealth in England.[19] Since secure alternatives to the employment of legally questionable future interests existed for almost the entire period, a more comprehensive examination of the settlements of the landowning classes in the sixteenth century must be undertaken before we can assert with confidence that a large number of inheritances were uncertain.

With these reservations in mind, we may now turn to a consideration of the land law with respect to restraints on alienation. After a consideration of contemporary views on the matter, the developing case law with regard to contingent remainders and executory interests will be discussed. In the succeeding chapter, an investigation of the forms employed in Kent and Northamptonshire in the first sixty years of the seventeenth century will be undertaken to consider the impact of these developments on conveyancing practice.

I

The function of the inheritance custom of primogeniture in preserving the general well-being of society in England was cogently expressed by Matthew Hale in his *History of the common law*. For the reverse, the division of inheritances, he argued: 'weakened the Strength of the Kingdom for by frequent parcelling and subdividing of Inheritances, in Process of Time they became so divided and crumbled, that there were few persons of able Estates left to undergo publick Charges and Offices.'[20] In short, the meshing of landed wealth with legal and administrative duties required a system of inheritance which promoted a stable ruling

---

18 J. P. Cooper, 'The social distribution of land and men in England 1436–1700', *Econ. Hist. Rev.*, 2nd ser. XX (1967), 422–3.

19 F. M. L. Thompson, 'The social distribution of landed property in England since the sixteenth century', *Econ. Hist. Rev.*, 2nd ser. XIX (1966), 514.

20 Matthew Hale, *The history of the common law of England*, ed. Charles M. Gray (Chicago, 1971), 142.

class; entail and primogeniture provided the legal framework for the preservation of this elite.[21]

While few seventeenth-century jurists opposed the concept of a well-ordered hierarchical society, juridical opinion was mixed regarding the efficacy of entails in accomplishing stability. In considering the broader ramifications Sir Francis Bacon discussed militating familial, economic and legal consequences. First, regarding their effect on the structure of the family, Bacon argued that entails bred sons who were 'disobedient, negligent and wasteful, often marrying without the Father's consent and growing insolent in vice knowing that there could be no check of disinheriting him'.[22] Secondly, in economic terms, Bacon concluded that entails prevented the landowner from raising the necessary capital from his tenants to improve his estate: because a tenant in tail could only grant an effective lease for his life, 'none on so uncertain an estate . . . would give him a fine of any value'.[23] In addition to leading to economic stagnation, there were further economic and legal considerations. Entails allowed creditors, including the Crown, to be defrauded because land in tail was not chargeable for personal debts of the tenant after his death. Perhaps most significantly, however, entails discouraged purchasers because one could not be certain of the seller's right to convey. Finally, Bacon contended that landowners were emboldened, that is, more inclined toward treason and felony, because they knew that their misdeeds would not jeopardize the descent of the patrimony.[24]

Bacon's professional and personal rival, Sir Edward Coke, concurred. Entails according to Coke were an unwelcome addition to the common law: 'by the wisdom of the Common law all estates

---

21 In addition to the debate on entails, a parallel controversy concerning primogeniture occurred in England in the sixteenth and seventeenth centuries. See Joan Thirsk, 'The European debate on customs of inheritance, 1500–1700', in *Family and inheritance*. Thirsk concludes that primogeniture was becoming more widespread in the sixteenth century.

22 *The use of the law*, 46. Some doubt exists as to whether the work should be attributed to Bacon.

23 *Ibid.*

24 *Ibid.* Many of these 'inconveniences' were remedied by statute: 4 Hen. VII c. 24 and 32 Hen. VII c. 28 allowed landowners to disinherit their sons by levying a fine with proclamations; 26 Hen. VII c. 13, entails forfeited for treasons; 32 Hen. VII c. 28, tenant in tail may make leases for twenty-one years or three lives; 33 Hen. VIII c. 2, entails liable to King's debt. By the mid-sixteenth century, therefore, there were only two 'privileges' remaining: (1) they were not forfeited for felony; and (2) they were not subject to the personal debts of the tenant after his death.

of inheritance were fee simple and what contentions and mischiefs have crept into the quiet of the law by these fettered inheritances, dailie experience teacheth us'.[25] As Coke noted, it was parliamentary interference with the land law, the statute *De donis*,[26] which was responsible for the alleged 'contentions and mischiefs'; and it is therefore appropriate to consider its origins and provisions. The provenance of the statute is obscure, and its proper construction was the subject of controversy in the fourteenth century.[27] It directs that the will of the donor in creating conditional fees shall be observed and 'when a tenant in tail maketh such discontinuance, he doth contrary to that'.[28] The extent to which entails were actually respected in the Middle Ages is unclear. Examples of their flouting clearly exist, although it has been suggested that most were allowed to run their course.[29] Whether the courts should continue to respect the desires of donors was very much a moot point in the sixteenth century. At least as early as 1472 the common law courts had sanctioned the barring of entails by a collusive law suit, the common recovery.[30] Some contemporary opinion considered that the motive of great magnates in rendering entails inalienable was 'for exalting and magnyfying of theyr owne blode: and therefore they say that that Statute made by suche a presumpcyon byndyth not in Conseyence'.[31]

If the common lawyers generally opposed entails, not all juridical opinion concurred. Christopher St German did not consider the statute *De donis* to be against the law of God or reason, nor did he believe that 'corrupt intent' vitiated the statute. Indeed, he appeared to favour the use of entails.[32] What troubled him was

25 *Co. Litt.*, 196.
26 13 Edw. I c. 1.
27 Milsom, *Historical foundations*, 175–8.
28 *Litt.*, 363.
29 J. M. W. Bean, *The estates of the Percy family, 1416–1537* (Cambridge, 1958), 121; Cooper, 'Patterns of inheritance', 201.
30 See footnote 9 above.
31 *Doctor and student*, 91, 159. Thomas Egerton concurred. A manual following reports of the Lord Keeper's decisions in Chancery relates: 'My Lord Keeper Saith that the statute . . . de Donis Conditionalibus was made but upon a singularity of conceit and that it had been well for the commonwealth if it had never been made': 'Observations in Course of Chauncery practice', C.U.L. MS Gg.ii. 31., fo. 466, section 216.
32 *Doctor and student*, 155–9. Mr Cooper ('Patterns of inheritance', 202) implied that St German opposed entails *per se*. For the reasons given below, I believe his view cannot stand.

not the restrictive nature of the interest but that the courts had sanctioned a collusive legal action to bar them. It was for this reason that he proposed that entails 'shulde hensforth eyther be made so stronge in the lawe that the tayle shude not be broken . . . or els that all tayles shude be made fee symple'.[33] Moreover, St German believed that even if entails were inconvenient the courts were not the proper forum to abolish them. Rather it was for parliament to rectify the consequences of *De donis*.[34]

In addition to mixed juristic opinion on entails, it is not altogether clear that the landed class favoured them. An abortive bill of 1529–30 and a subsequent agreement between the Crown and thirty peers may well indicate that the peerage refused an offer of unbarrable entails. Although the origin of the bill is disputed, the extant draft would have abolished entails and converted them into estates in fee simple with the exception of the land owned by peers.[35] Henceforth all the estates of the peers could be alienated only with royal licence. The absence of such a provision in the agreement subsequently proposed regarding feudal incidents has apparently led Professor Stone to the conclusion that these peers refused the offer of secure entails.[36] However, Dr Ives has argued that the measure was essentially one dealing with land registration, and that the provisions concerning entails were an afterthought.[37] It is therefore contended that the bill was not related to the subsequent agreement, and that the magnates capitulated to avoid the 'full terror of fiscal feudalism'.[38] Because the documents were unrelated in purpose, there was no provision concerning unbarrable entails for the peers in the agreement. On the other hand, Professor Bean

33 *Doctor and student*, 173.
34 'yf in yt case there be lyke auctorytie in the makynge of the tayle as there is in the adnullynge thereof/for it was ordayned by auctorytie of Parlyament/the whiche is always taken for the most hyghe courte in this realme before any other . . .' *Ibid.*, 159–60.
35 Both the bill and the agreement are in *H.E.L.*, IV, 572–7. Holdsworth (*ibid.*, 450) considers the bill official and G. R. Elton ('Parliamentary drafts, 1529–1540', *B.I.H.R.*, XXV (1952), 132) agrees. Bean (*English feudalism*) concurs, while E. W. Ives ('The genesis of the Statute of Uses', *E.H.R.*, LXXXII (1967)) denies official provenance.
36 Lawrence Stone, *The crisis of the aristocracy, 1558–1641* (Oxford, 1965), 182.
37 Ives, 'Genesis', 680. The layout of the bill, and especially the fact that the provision abolishing comes first, cast some doubt on Dr Ives's conclusion. However, it seems equally clear that the bill deals primarily with the evils of secret conveyances.
38 *Ibid.*, 681.

has argued that the two documents were connected, but that the aristocracy refused the offer because entails served no purpose since their settlements were effected by way of use.[39] Thus neither the bill nor the agreement would have deprived any landowner, peer or gentleman, of the power to create restraints upon alienation by employing equitable estates; what the agreement would have achieved for the Crown was to render such settlements financially less desirable.

Neither of these views, however, is necessarily inconsistent with Professor Stone's conclusion. Even if there was no connection between the two documents, it is likely that the thirty peers were aware of the draft bill. Had they treasured the notion of a privileged mode of inheritance for their rank, it would have been a small concession for the Crown to have granted it, considering the onerous financial exactions of the agreement. Perhaps the peers did not relish the thought of their heirs petitioning the Crown each time it was necessary or desirable for them to alienate land. Moreover, since neither the bill nor the agreement would have deprived the landowner of the power to create restraints upon alienation by way of use, there was little tangible incentive for the peers to insist upon unbarrable entails save for vanity.

For whatever reason, the aspirations of St German, to rationalize the law with regard to entails by means of a parliamentary act, never came to fruition. The subsequent Statute of Uses[40] had no effect upon entails of legal estates, but it did tend to shift the focus of settlors towards settlements employing equitable interests.[41] Nevertheless, common lawyers continued their invectives against entails. In discussing statutory modifications of the common law, William Noy reckoned that the Statute De donis did 'much more harm than good to the Commonwealth and Subjects';[42] and William Sheppard flatly asserted 'That Entails upon land is inconvenient'.[43] Yet suggestions for new forms of entail which in practice might be unbarrable continue to appear in the seventeenth

39 Bean, English feudalism, 259. Bean argues that it was 'more likely that the promise that entails would be confined to their class was intended as a sop to the pride of the nobility'.
40 27 Hen. VIII c. 10.
41 See below, pp. 35–45.
42 William Noy, The complete lawyer or a treatise concerning tenures (London, 1651), 31.
43 William Sheppard, England's balme (London, 1657), 215.

century. Sheppard cites a case of 1662 in which the Court of King's Bench considered that a gift of an entail upon condition that 'the donee shall pay £10 to the donor if he attempts to bar the entail', was good.[44] Even so vehement an opponent of entails as Coke could propose ingenious forms of restraints on alienation: 'A seised in fee of Blackacre is enfeoffed of Whiteacre by B upon condition that A shall not alien Blackacre'; because it was annexed to other land, this condition was valid since it 'ousteth not the feoffee of his power to alien the land whereof the feoffment is made, and so no repugnancy to the estate passed by the feoffment'.[45] Thus in the minds of some lawyers the possibility of devising conditions which rendered land inalienable had not ceased, despite the use of the common recovery to bar entails.

The upheaval of the mid-seventeenth century witnessed a fresh spate of agitation for law reform, including the call for the abolition of entails, but the attack focused upon the inconvenience and expense of barring them rather than upon any consideration of morality or egalitarianism. Sheppard attacked the existing system of conveyancing, objecting that the 'profits of them by Fines, Recoveries and Deeds, are very troublesome, chargeable and dangerous'; he suggested that a simple fine with subsequent local registration should be sufficient to bar an entail.[46] Estates of the lesser landowners were often likewise entailed, raising financial problems. Urging that a deed of bargain and sale should be deemed as strong as a fine and recovery, John Cook commented: 'if a poor Farmer or Cottager might leave some small portions to his younger children without paying one or two years purchase for the charge of a fine and recovery, what an ease this might be to men of small estates to passe them from one to another and cut off entails by deed in writing without so much solemnite and expence'.[47] Legal procedure had created onerous burdens for the small landowner.

In response to demands made by the army for a general enquiry

44 *Bragg and Tanner's Case*, Pasc. 19 Jac. B.R., cited in William Sheppard, *The touchstone of common assurances* (London, 1651), 130. From the report in Cro. Jac. 596 it would appear that this point was *dicta*.
45 *Co. Litt.*, 223a.
46 Sheppard, *England's balme*, 215.
47 John Cook, *Monarchy no creature of God's making* (Waterford, 1651), 26. Hale noted that to sell an acre of land necessitated a fine and recovery which cost about 50s. Matthew Hale, *A treatise concerning the enrollment of deeds* (London, 1694), 21.

into the substantive and procedural law, Parliament appointed an independent committee 'to take into Consideration what inconveniencies there are in the Law, and how the Mischiefs that grow from the delays may be prevented'.[48] A recent appraisal contends that the composition of the extra-parliamentary committee, the Hale Commission as it came to be known, was moderate but with a radical minority.[49] Regardless, the highly technical level of the debate insured that members of the legal profession would dominate the proceedings.[50] With regard to land law, a consensus favoured procedural reform,[51] and a draft statute emerged which would have in effect abolished the distinction between entails and estates in fee simple.[52] Moreover, the measure would have corrected the second most frequently discussed abuse by rendering an entailed estate liable for the personal debts of the tenant in tail after his death.[53]

It must, however, be noted that there is no record of any debate regarding the economic or social consequences of rendering land inalienable by the employment of entails and perpetuities. Nor does it appear that their outright abolition by statute was proposed. Because the committee was dominated by moderate lawyers, its main concern with regard to the land law was to simplify conveyancing procedure. In practice, the courts had already adopted a policy of free alienation of real property, and what needed tidying were the more practical aspects.[54] Consequently, the absence of any discussion of restraints upon alienation in the minutes of the Hale Commission, and the focus upon procedural rather than substantive reform in the proposed statute, should come as no surprise.

Up to this point, this discussion of contemporary comment with regard to restraints on alienation has been confined to entails. During this period, however, controversy raged over a different

48 C.J., VI, 58: 26 December 1651. A parliamentary committee already existed, but it was considered by the army to be dominated by conservative lawyers.
49 M. Cotterell, 'Interregnum law reform: the Hale Commission of 1652', E.H.R., LXXXIII (1968), 691–4.
50 A clerk was present at the meetings of the commission and the minutes remain: B.L., Hardwicke MS 35863. Much of the manuscript is difficult to read, and some of the accounts appear sketchy.
51 Ibid., fos. 77–81.
52 The text appears in Somers's tracts, 2nd edn (London, 1811), 6, 182–3. The first clause of the proposed bill would allow entails to be conveyed by bargain and sale.
53 Ibid., 183, clause 3.
54 See below, pp. 42–5.

form of restraint, the perpetuity: 'men did entail their lands with this condition That none of them that had the Land by the Entail, should do an Act to put it from the next Heir, and if he did that he should forfeit his Estate and that the next heir should enter upon him'.[55] The origins of clauses of perpetuity are obscure. Some lawyers believed that the device was developed after statutory provisions alleviated many of the abuses of entails.[56] Modern research, however, disputes this theory.[57] Whatever their origins, it was argued that 'if they should stand they would bring in all the former inconveniences subject to entails'.[58] Coke contended that the device, like any innovation, should be tested by the rules of the common law 'for these be true touchstones to sever the pure gold from the drosse'.[59] By this standard, perpetuities would fail because the common law had never recognized the validity of a remainder to take effect after an estate forfeited for breach of condition.

For the most part arguments similar to those advanced against entails were directed at perpetuities. With the incidence of primogeniture increasing amongst the landed class during the sixteenth century, and a concomitant increase of concern for the rigours which it imposed upon younger sons, an additional point was raised.[60] Where the patrimony was free from restraints upon alienation, fathers might more effectively provide for their younger sons, and raise portions for their daughters either by *inter vivos* transfer or by testament. Perpetuities deprived landowners of their power to do so; accordingly, 'they must suffer the whole to descend to the eldest Sonne, and so come to the Crowne by Wardship'.[61]

55 William Sheppard, *An epitome of all the common and statute laws of the nation* (London, 1656), 796.
56 *Use of the law*, 47. Note also Bacon's argument in *Chudleigh's Case*, where he stated that the form had been used for sixty years: Bacon, *Works*, VII, 491. An anonymous manuscript entitled 'Concerning entayles and perpetuities' concludes: 'After all this care taken against entayles . . . Yet did the weavers of their own Wills set upp an unwelcomed guest called a Perpetuity . . . [which] undertook to repair the decline of his parent and to uphold houses in greater Pompe than ever before could be.' B.L., Lansdowne MS 216, fos. 58–9.
57 Cooper, 'Patterns of inheritance', 204.
58 *Use of the law*, 47.
59 *Co. Litt.*, 379b.
60 Thirsk, 'European debate', 183–5. In addition to the literary evidence cited by Dr Thirsk, the statutory disgavelling of the estates of particular landowners in Kent (31 Hen. VIII c. 3 and 32 Hen. VIII c. 29) and the wholesale disgavelling of Wales (27 Hen. VIII c. 26) are evidence of the increased acceptance of primogeniture.
61 *Use of the law*, 48.

Thus perpetuities removed from the landowner the modicum of freedom of disposition conceded by the Statute of Wills.[62] Furthermore, perpetuities were attacked for the contentions which they spawned in a society marked by litigiousness. Innovation was rarely favoured by the common law, precisely because it engendered controversy. As Coke noted: 'ancient judges and sages of the law have ever suppressed innovation and novelties in the beginning as soon as they have offered to creepe up, lest the quiet of the common law might be disturbed'.[63] Coke vigorously opposed judicial acceptance, while Bacon argued that perpetuities fostered lawsuits between relatives over a pittance with resultant legal costs so onerous 'that in the end they are both constrained by necessity to joyne in the sale of the land . . . to pay their debts'.[64] Indeed, Bacon contended that the uncertainty over the law with regard to perpetuities may have prompted settlors to employ them: 'in the meantime if they prove void, yet the law varies as it chance and will be a bridle on the heir that he shall not venture to sell and a scruple to the purchaser that he shall not buy, and so it is but an conveyance adventured, inconvenience there is none'.[65] Essentially, to employ perpetuities, 'nothing ventured nothing gained'; if the restraint proved invalid at law, the heir merely gained the same power of disposition incident to any estate of inheritance which the settlor could initially have conveyed.

Contemporary comment regarding entails and perpetuities will again be considered in investigating the development of case law, since the judges were strongly influenced by policy considerations in determining which forms of settlement were valid. Fortunately for the legal historian they were not reluctant to express their views in their opinions. But the validity of perpetuities was initially admitted. To understand why, it may be apposite to recall the apology for entails and primogeniture offered by Hale. Clearly, he was not isolated in his view; even so vehement an opponent of restraints upon alienation as Bacon conceded: 'therefore it is worthy of consideration, whether it be better for the subject and Sovereigns to have the lands secured to mens names and bloods by perpetuities with all the inconveniences above mentioned, or to be

62 32 Hen. VII c. 1.
63 *Co. Litt.*, 379a.
64 *Use of the law*, 47.
65 *Works*, VII, 623.

in hazard of undoing his house by unthrifty posterity'.[66] Perhaps it was this dilemma, whether the political and social stability which entails and perpetuities appeared to foster and the possible upheaval which free alienability might engender outweighed the inconveniences, which explains the hesitancy of the common law to invalidate long-term restraints upon alienation. While the common law courts were equivocating on the issue of the effect of the Statute of Uses on executory interests, the judges were relaxing some of the rigours of the law of contingent remainders to allow those settlors with less grandiose designs for their patrimonies to effect more secure settlements. It is to these developments that we may now turn.

II

The transformation of many of the future interests which could be created by the machinery of the use into legal estates by the Statute of Uses, coupled with the broad power of disposition over real property conceded by the Statute of Wills, seemed to offer those who sought to restrain alienation of the patrimony long after their deaths an opportunity to effect their designs. But when cases arose in the common law courts which involved the validity of contingent remainders and executory interests, some of the judges, in their endeavour to discourage the creation of settlements which restrained alienation, took the position that no estate which would be invalid at common law could take effect by way of use executed by the statute.[67] Their primary concern was to limit the ability of landowners to fetter inheritances; had this position been established their aim would have been achieved. For by treating both sorts of interests similarly, the common law courts could limit the possibility of creating lengthy settlements by the employment of legal executory interests in the same manner as they controlled the dangers inherent in the manipulation of contingent remainders: by assessing the impact of each innovation, and then carefully choosing which limitations were valid.

While in the end this extreme position did not prevail, it did have the effect of bringing the contingent remainder into prominence,

66 *Use of the law*, 49.
67 Coke expounded this view as an advocate in *Chudleigh's Case* (1595), 1 Co. Rep. 120a, 129a. Popham, C. J. also subscribed to this view: 1 Co. Rep. 120a, 138.

since those who wished to discountenance restraints upon alienation would argue that what could be effected by contingent remainder was the outer limit of what could be effected by legal executory interests. Although most landowners in the reign of Elizabeth appear to have been willing to settle vested entails upon the prospective bride and groom, some settlors began to turn to the use of contingent remainders to effect a more complex disposition. The aim of these settlements was similar to those which granted entails: to provide a competent jointure and to transmit the patrimony to the next generation. But the manipulation of contingent remainders had a further distinct advantage, because the settlor might circumscribe the power of the groom to alienate by limiting in him a lesser estate. However, the attempt to do so could be successful only if the court protected the interests created. During the latter half of the sixteenth and the early seventeenth centuries, cases arose in the common law courts in which questions concerning the validity of contingent remainders were resolved, allowing for their employment in marriage settlements.

In particular, there were four developments. First, the decision in *Colethirst* v. *Bejushin*[68] enabled the landowner to employ alternative contingent remainders in marriage settlements which would ensure that the patrimony descended to his eldest son in tail, or, if he predeceased his parents, to a younger son so long as both were living at the time of settlement. Secondly, the court in *Wild's Case*[69] confirmed that a gift over to children after a grant to their parents might take effect by way of remainder even though the children were not *in esse* at the time of the devise, thereby facilitating the execution of pre-nuptial settlements.[70] Thirdly, the common law courts undertook to protect settlements of short-term duration from certain of the rigours of the rules of destructibility by modifying the rule in *Shelley's Case*.[71] Finally, the courts endeavoured to construe remainders in settlements which did not tend towards perpetuities as vested rather than as contingent if such an interpretation was at all possible.

68 (1551), Plowden 21.
69 (1599), 6 Co. Rep. 16b.
70 Although *Wild's Case* concerns a devise and the decision turns on the intent of the testator, the rationale and examples given apply as well to grants. Coke discusses the principle in the *Institutes* in terms of grants. *Co. Litt.*, 9a.
71 (1579), 1 Co. Rep. 88b.

Consequently, in settlements employing these interests in accordance with the above decisions, the contingent remainder began to provide a 'safe harbour' for those settlors unwilling to dabble in perpetuities and other executory interests of dubious validity. Whether these decisions actually encouraged the use of the sanctioned forms may be open to question. While it is not possible to demonstrate a link between court decisions and changes in settlement practice, it is not unreasonable to infer a causal connection where conveyancing practice followed developments in legal doctrine. The legal profession in early modern England was after all rather small and centralized. It is therefore reasonable to suggest that it was from these decisions that a distinct pattern of marriage settlement evolved from which, after the insertion of trustees to preserve contingent remainders in the mid-seventeenth century, the fully fledged strict settlement emerged.

Before turning in more detail to these cases, it may be helpful to outline the principles relevant to conveyancing practice and applicable to legal remainders in the decades after the Statute of Uses. The first principle was that a remainder must await the regular termination of the precedent estate. In effect, the rule prevented a remainder from determining its supporting estate prematurely; it was a condition, as opposed to a limitation, which could determine an estate before its natural end.[72] Secondly, it was established that a freehold could not be limited to arise *in futuro*; or as Littleton expressed the rule: 'no remainder may be limited to take effect upon the expiration of an interval of time after the determination of the preceding estate'.[73] Supporting this rule was the underlying legal requirement that there could be no abeyance of seisin. When, therefore, the validity of a contingent remainder to the heirs of a living person was first admitted, it was only recognized if the heir was ascertained by the death of that person before the termination of the preceding estate.[74] And finally, it was held that the remainder must pass from the grantor at the same time as livery of seisin of its supporting estate was accomplished.[75]

Because of the fear that contingent remainders might be

---

72 That this rule was long accepted is clear from *Colethirst* v. *Bejushin* (1551), Plowden 21.
73 *Litt.*, 60.
74 Y.B. 9 Hen. VI, Trin., 42, pl. 19.
75 *Colethirst* v. *Bejushin* (1551), Plowden 21.

employed to create lengthy settlements, the common law courts formulated a number of other requirements which applied exclusively to these interests. By far the most important was that the estate which supported a contingent remainder must be a freehold interest.[76] The legal rationale supporting this rule was once again related to the problem of seisin: if the supporting estate was not a freehold, where would seisin lie pending the occurrence of the contingency? Such a problem did not arise with vested remainders, because seisin vested in the remainderman at the time of the conveyance. The practical effect of this rule was that a contingent remainder could not be limited to take effect after a term of years. Long leases were both a common and a valuable interest; the uncertainty, and later the flexibility, of the contingent remainder did not apply to leasehold estates.

A corollary to this rule recognized that in a conveyance of a freehold followed by a contingent remainder, the contingent remainder must vest or fail before or upon the termination of its supporting freehold estate. Such a requirement, that an interest must vest or fail within a certain period of time, was a step towards the modern rule against perpetuities. However, it was only applied negatively; that is, it illustrated what could not be done, and a conveyance with contingent interests might still be held invalid even though the contingencies had to occur or fail within a fixed period of time.[77]

If by its terms the contingent remainder did not operate within these rules, the interest would not be protected by the law; or as contemporary lawyers would say, it was 'destroyed'. For the most part, these rules of destructibility of contingent remainders were successful in frustrating attempts to create lengthy settlements in legal estates. While the law with regard to contingent remainders developed slowly, it is clear that by the third quarter of the sixteenth century the courts were taking a more lenient attitude towards the destructibility of contingent remainders, especially where it was apparent that they were not being employed to create long-term restraints upon alienation. With these rules of destructibility firmly in mind we may now turn in more detail to these developments in the case law.

76 *Butler* v. *Bray* (1561), Dyer 189.
77 Note the settlement set aside in *Child* v. *Bailie* (1618), Cro. Jac. 59, and *Jay* v. *Jay* (1651), Style 258.

The first type of contingent remainder recognized at common law was one based upon the death of a living person. Since the common law had long assumed the position that a living person had no heirs, a conveyance 'to A for life, with remainder to the heirs of B' was, if B was living, a gift of a remainder to an unascertained person; and it was held that the gift over was void *ab initio*. However, recognizing the cruel inevitability of death, the common law began to allow the remainder to take effect if the heir was identified before the termination of the supporting estate; that is, if B died within the lifetime of A.[78] With regard to marriage settlements, the decision was a significant one, because upon the marriage of his son (in this case B) a settlor might now be able to secure an entail in his grandson (the heir of B) should he survive his own son (B). Such a contingency was not as remote as might appear at first glance given the demographic climate of sixteenth-century England.

Later, however, remainders based upon contingencies other than the death of a living person were likewise admitted. In this regard *Colethirst* v. *Bejushin* has been considered a landmark case in the common law courts' move towards greater flexibility in its treatment of contingent remainders.[79] It may be useful to discuss it in detail, because counsel and the judges argued the case at length and appear to have disagreed upon the nature of the interest created by the settlement. In particular, two subtleties arose with regard to the validity of the contingent remainder conveyed, which in substance ran as follows: 'to husband and wife for their lives, the remainder to elder son for life, but if he dies living the husband and wife and then to younger son'.[80] The first contention was related to the highly technical question of when, if ever, seisin passed to the younger son. Serjeant Pollard, arguing against the validity of the remainder over, considered that it must be void because the condition, the elder son predeceasing his parents, preceded the remainder to the younger son; therefore, the supporting estate must have been created before the contingent remainder, and con-

78 Y.B. 9 Hen. VII, Trin., 23, pl. 19.
79 *H.E.L.*, VII, 87.
80 The eldest son died in the lifetime of his parents and the issue joined was whether the remainder to the younger son was good. A second issue arose concerning a condition annexed to the enjoyment of the estate concerning the furnishing of hospitality, but this was resolved and had no bearing on the validity of the remainder.

sequently seisin could not have passed to him when it passed to his parents. Secondly, even granting that seisin passed to the younger son simultaneously with its passage to the husband and wife, he argued that the condition was not one which the law should deem valid.

Pollard's subtlety regarding seisin was rejected by the judges. It was agreed that seisin passed to the younger son when the grant was made, but the estate was held in abeyance. Justice Hales noted that 'when livery is made . . . and thereupon words are spoken, there by force of such words and some act afterwards done a freehold may be passed from one to another'.[81] But if seisin passed immediately there was disagreement as to when the estate passed to the younger son. Hales argued that the remainder did not pass to the younger son until the death of his elder brother, and that it did not vest until the death of his parents. Consequently, seisin could pass before the estate was in existence. Chief Justice Mountague did not accept such a radical view. He believed that the estate passed out of the grantor immediately, and was thereafter in abeyance until the performance of the condition 'in respect of the possibility that it might be performed'.[82] Hales and Mountague also disagreed regarding the time at which the estate in the younger son vested. According to Hales the estate vested upon the death of the parents, while Mountague argued that it vested upon the death of the elder son. Despite these significant differences, it was clear that the validity of contingent remainders was not to be affected by the actual wording of grants. Niceties of form were not to thwart the intent of settlors so long as the interests created were legitimate.

The report suggests that there was a further diversity of opinion. The judges disagreed as to whether the grant to the younger son commenced upon a condition. Mountague believed that it did. Citing a year book case from the reign of Henry VIII where an entail was granted 'To A upon condition that A and his heirs carried S's standard in battle, and if they failed to do so, to B', Mountague considered it to be settled law that a freehold may pass by condition where it was expressed at the time when livery of the supporting estate was made.[83] Justice Hinde, however, denied that the estate in the younger son was conditional. Conditions, he argued, restrained

81 Plowden 21, 31.
82 *Ibid.*, at 35.
83 *Ibid.*, at 34. The year book case is Y.B. 27 Hen. VIII, Mich., 24, pl. 2.

what was granted; the words here were an explanation of the time when the remainder was to commence, and therefore must be a limitation. Rules of law regarding limitations were more flexible than those touching conditions. Accordingly, a limitation might be effected to direct that an estate commence at any time during the life of its supporting estate. Thus, despite differing opinions on the passing of seisin, the time at which the estate vested and the nature of the words which brought the estate into being, the court held the settlement to be valid. For the first time, the common law sanctioned the employment of alternative contingent remainders, ignoring Pollard's eloquent plea concerning the havoc which would be brought if the validity of those interests were to be extended: 'And further my Lords, it is to be considered and observed that in every Weal-Public it is necessary and requisite that the conveyance of things should be certain for certainty is the Mother of Repose and Incertainty the Mother of Contention, which our wise and provident law has ever guarded against and prevents all occasions thereof.'[84]

Two other separate though interrelated points regarding seisin were raised in the case; and although they seem at first glance not to have had a bearing upon the outcome, they may serve as harbingers of future developments with regard to contingent remainders. Hales first noted that by allowing the alternative remainder, there was no 'prejudice to a stranger'; that is to say the remainder in the younger son did not defeat a pre-existing estate.[85] Secondly, Serjeant Saunders argued that seisin of the remainder limited to the younger son could be considered *in pendenti*: 'And in as much as the Son is able to take the Possession in Law at the Time when it is cast and fallen the remainder shall be good enough.'[86] Thus it was argued that if there was no defeasance a remainder might be limited to an unborn person and be held in abeyance. Such a view goes a long way towards accepting in principle the concept of the strict settlement where trustees protect the interest pending the vesting of the remainder without defeating a pre-existing interest.

Turning now to *Wild's Case*,[87] where this last point was again considered, it was adjudged in the King's Bench that land devised

84 Plowden 21, 25.
85 *Ibid.*, 31.
86 *Ibid.*, 29.
87 *Ibid.*, 17b.

'to husband and wife and after to their children' should be construed as a valid gift of a contingent remainder to the children. Accordingly, it was irrelevant that no son was *in esse* at the time of conveyance: 'Yet every child which they may have after may take by remainder, according to the rule of the law; for his intent appears that their children should not take immediately but after the death of Rowland and his wife.'[88] Consequently, the types of acceptable contingent remainders were broadened to include limitations to unborn persons. Where the expressed intent was for a remainder to be enjoyed in the future, the remainderman need not be *in esse* at the time of the settlement. So long as remaindermen were described sufficiently and were in existence at the time when the estate was to vest the remainder was valid. Such a view could only be countenanced if estates *in pendenti* were generally accepted. While the court did not consider the acceptable period during which postponement was to be allowed, the period between marriage and the birth of an heir was sanctioned. Applying similar principles to other grants, such as marriage settlements, a limitation of a life estate to the married couple, followed by remainder in tail in the eldest son produced by the marriage, secured a recognizable interest in the eldest son. Pre-nuptial marriage settlements of this variety were henceforth more secure.

In addition to sanctioning a wider variety of acceptable contingencies, therefore, the judges were elaborating a more flexible trend in legal doctrine which was increasingly favourable to the execution of marriage settlements. Yet important distinctions between vested and contingent remainders continued to be drawn. The interest, while contingent, was only of potential rather than present value. It was virtually an unmarketable commodity being held inalienable either *inter vivos* or by will.[89] This position came to be relaxed by the close of the sixteenth century when it was held that a contingent remainderman could release his interest to the tenant in possession[90] or bar it by levying a fine.[91]

Most significantly, however, until the device of trustees to preserve contingent remainders was contrived, the contingent

88 (1559), 6 Co. Rep. 16b.
89 *Lampet's Case* (1613), 10 Co. Rep. 46b, 48a; *H.E.L.*, VII, 103.
90 *Lampet's Case* (1613), 10 Co. Rep. 46b, 48a.
91 *Powle* v. *Veare* (1599), Moo. K.B. 554. It was not until the eighteenth century that contingent executory devices could be alienated. See Charles Fearne, *An essay on the learning of contingent remainders*, 7th edn (London, 1820), 5–7.

remainder was an extremely precarious interest, because legal principles governing seisin and merger enabled a party to the settlement to destroy it. In practice, this could be accomplished by a tortious feoffment, or by a fine or recovery. In addition, a disseisin of the life tenant could destroy contingent remainders supported by that life estate; though the right of entry held by the disseised life tenant could still support the contingent remainder, once a descent occurred the interest in his heir was converted to a right of action which could not support the remainder.[92] Moreover, under the principles of merger, the conveyance of reversion to the life tenant, or the reverse, would destroy any contingent remainders which were supported by the life estate.[93] Likewise, the surrender of the life interest to a vested remainderman would also destroy the contingent remainder.[94]

While the above examples demonstrate that the contingent remainder could easily be destroyed by actions of the tenant in possession, it could in some instances be defeated without the connivance of parties to the settlement. As a result of the operation of the rule in *Shelley's Case*,[95] the merger of the precedent estate and the next vested estate of inheritance would destroy dependent contingent remainders. A simple descent might result in merger of two interests. For example, testator seised in fee devises 'to eldest son for life with remainder in tail to the successive sons of that son'; here the estate for life and the next vested estate of inheritance (the reversion in fee simple) would simultaneously vest in the eldest son, the former by will and the latter by descent.[96]

To rescue the intent of the settlor, the common law courts by the third quarter of the sixteenth century undertook to avoid the consequences of the law of merger by disregarding the rule in *Shelley's Case* where it found the intent to create two separate interests sufficiently clear. Curiously enough, this position, a third step towards facilitating the employment of contingent remainders in marriage settlements, first came in a case regarding a testamentary disposition, and one in which the court reinforced the

92 *Thompson v. Leach* (1697), 12 Mod. 173.
93 *Purefoy v. Rogers* (1671), 2 Wm. Saunders 380.
94 *Thompson v. Leach* (1697), 12 Mod. 173.
95 (1579), 1 Co. Rep. 93b.
96 H. W. Challis, *Law of real property*, 3rd edn (London, 1911), 135–6.

precarious nature of contingent remainders.[97] Land was devised 'to A for life and then to his next heir male'; since A was the heir at law to the testator, the fee descended upon him causing his life estate to merge into the fee, thereby destroying the contingent remainder to his heirs. The court, however, held that the intent of the testator was to create two separate interests, a life estate in A and a contingent remainder in his right heir. Yet the decision offered no comfort to landowners, since the court further determined that the remainder could vest only upon the death of A, in accordance with the position at common law that a person had no heirs until his death. Therefore, it was held that a feoffment by the life tenant would destroy the remainder because it was contingent, even though he had a son at the time of the conveyance. A similar position was taken with respect to marriage settlements. In *Lewis Bowles's Case*[98] the court held that a conveyance 'to husband and wife for their lives with remainder to their heirs male in succession' created in the married couple 'an estate tail executed *sub modo* until the birth of issue male, and then by operation of law the estates are divided . . . and Thomas and Anne [husband and wife] become tenants for their lives with remainders to the issue male in tail . . .'[99] Although the contingent remainder could be destroyed by the tenant in possession, the relaxation of the rule in *Shelley's Case* facilitated the execution of marriage settlements where landowners were content to trust the discretion of their heir male.[100]

Had these exceptions not been admitted, settlements employing contingent remainders would often have failed to pass land into the next generation. But the common law courts were quite willing to sanction contingent remainders such as the ones limited in *Archer's Case* and *Lewis Bowles's Case*, where the intent of the landowner was to effect a settlement of limited duration; and as the cases above suggest, the courts did allow some degree of flexibility to accom-

97 *Archer's Case* (1597), 1 Co. Rep. 66a. The rule in *Archer's Case* appears to reverse the position regarding the destructibility of contingent remainders by fine with proclamations in *Humfreston's Case*, Dyer 337a. See generally, Barton, 'Future interests and royal revenues'.
98 (1616), 11 Co. Rep. 79b.
99 *Ibid.*
100 *Co. Litt.*, 28a. Succeeding cases reinforced the principle that the life tenant could destroy the contingent remainder even after the birth of a male child. The remainder continued to be considered contingent because of the common law rule that heirs were ascertainable only at death. *Chudleigh's Case* (1595), 1 Co. Rep. 120a, 135b; *Biggot* v. *Smith* (1627), Cro. Car. 102; *Napper* v. *Saunders* (1630), Hutton 119.

plish this goal. Moreover, under some circumstances the court often endeavoured to interpret a remainder as vested, thereby completely circumventing the rules of destructibility.[101] Settlements of long duration, however, were a different matter; and the judges rigorously enforced the rules of destructibility where the intent of the settlor was to fetter the patrimony for what they considered to be an unreasonable period. Indeed, *dicta* in *Chudleigh's Case*[102] implied that the rules of destructibility of contingent remainders should apply to contingent uses as well; and this extension of the rules of destructibility was precipitated by the fear of the common law judges that uses were being employed to create perpetuities.[103]

Thus certain developments in the law with regard to contingent remainders were not inimical to the landowner. So long as the settlor or the testator was content to control the devolution of the patrimony to the next generation only, the common law courts were increasingly inclined to honour his intentions by sanctioning and protecting various contingent remainders. The mode of settlement which evolved from these decisions will be illustrated below, but at this juncture it is appropriate to reiterate that, while sanctioning this degree of flexibility, the common law courts devised and adhered to a doctrine which was designed to insure that ambitious settlors did not take advantage of these developments to create settlements of long duration.

The doctrine enunciated, one of 'possibilities', allowed the judges to defeat remainders which were based upon contingencies which were considered to be too remote.[104] But the definition developed was hazy, and perhaps purposely so, because the doctrine supplied a technical reason to set aside settlements which fettered inheritances for more than a generation, while allowing the judges to uphold ones that did not. At first glance the rule appeared simple enough: 'a possibility which shall make a remainder good ought to be a common possibility, and *potentia propinqua* as death,

101 H. Finch, *Nottingham's Chancery cases*, ed. D. E. C. Yale (Selden Society, London, 1954), 73, 210. Case 301 cites such examples. See discussion in the editor's Introduction, lxxiv.
102 (1595), 1 Co. Rep. 120a.
103 See for example Lord Chancellor Hardwicke's opinion in *Garth* v. *Cotton* (1735), Dickens 183, 193 and discussion below, pp. 35–45.
104 For a complete treatment of the question see C. Sweet, 'Double possibilities', *Law Quarterly Review*, XXX (1914) and also his article in the *Yale Law Journal*, XXVII (1917).

or death without issue or coverture or the like'.[105] Yet this list was not meant to be exhaustive, and given the plethora of possible conditions, such a formulation could never constitute a viable prospective test for settlors.

What was necessary was to fix the outer limits of restraints upon alienation which could be implemented by contingent remainders. In the *Rector of Chedington's Case*,[106] Chief Justice Popham attempted to do so by holding that an interest could not commence upon a contingency which depended upon another contingency. Apparently no precedent existed for the distinction between what he called 'single' and 'double' possibilities,[107] but more significantly the test as applied was not a useful one to thwart restraints upon alienation, since there was no relationship between the probability of occurrence of the contingency and the time at which the remainder was to be enjoyed. Moreover, as Coke conceded, a strict literal enforcement of the doctrine would render nearly all common assurances void.[108] After the courts established the principle that any settlement which tended towards a perpetuity was void, the distinction between 'possibilities' was abandoned. Once this point was settled, the courts no longer found it necessary to focus upon the character of the limitation and began to fashion a rule based upon remoteness of vesting.

It was, however, innovative settlements employing executory interests which spurred the courts into adopting this principle. Because the ambiguous formulation of acceptable possibilities served to prevent the creation of long-term settlements by the manipulation of contingent remainders, settlors bent upon creating long-term settlements were driven to employing executory interests. But, as we turn to an investigation of the efforts of conveyancers in employing executory interests by way of use to effect such settlements, it is vital to note that the trend in legal doctrine with respect to contingent remainders was towards flexibility: to allow the intergenerational transfer of the patrimony by sanctioning various previously unaccepted interests, while at the same time preserving the policy against restraints upon alienation by adhering to the 'possibilities' test.

105 *Cholmley's Case* (1597), 2 Co. Rep. 50a, 51b.
106 (1598), 1 Co. Rep. 153b.
107 J. C. Gray, *The rule against perpetuities* (Boston, Mass., 1886), 125–33.
108 *Blamford* v. *Blamford* (1613), 1 Rolle. Rep. 321. Cf. *Co. Litt.*, 184a.

It has been noted that feoffments to uses were employed in marriage and family settlements in the later Middle Ages to fix jointures and to effect the hereditary disposition of real property.[109] After the enactment of the Statute of Uses in 1536, two distinct threads of juristic opinion emerged regarding its impact upon equitable future interests. Some lawyers believed that the purpose of the statute was primarily fiscal, and therefore that the flexibility of the use survived the statute. Perhaps this view was best put forward by Justice Manwood in *Brent's Case*: 'And although uses are of such antiquity yet they are not directed by the rules of common law, but by the will of the owner of the lands; for the use is in his hands as clay is in the hands of the potter, which he in whose hands it may be put into what form he pleaseth.'[110] Yet not all members of the profession subscribed to this view; the more zealous amongst the common lawyers concluded that the statute 'made an end of uses'.[111] For example, Chief Justice Popham in his opinion in *Chudleigh's Case* considered that uses were 'utterly extirpated and extinguished by this Act: for it appears by the express letter of the Act, that it was the intent of Parliament to extirpate and extinguish them and to restore the ancient common law of the land'.[112]

Neither of these extreme views prevailed, and in the end the danger which the use engendered, that it might be employed to create perpetuities, was resolved by establishing a rule based upon remoteness of vesting.[113] Until this approach to the problem was countenanced, however, the courts were faced with a spate of novel and ingenious conveyances which were designed to create enduring restraints upon alienation. Where uses were manipulated to effect perpetuities, they were after a period of judicial ambivalence held invalid.[114] Yet the common law courts accepted, albeit reluctantly, the flexibility of the use with respect to executory devises by

109 See above, pp. 1–10.
110 (1575), 2 Leon. 14, 16.
111 *Ibid.*, 15.
112 (1595), 1 Co. Rep. 120a, 138a.
113 This argument was adopted by Lord Nottingham in the *Duke of Norfolk's Case*, 3 Ch. Cas. 1 (1681), and is the essence of the modern rule against perpetuities. For the evolution of the rule up to Lord Nottingham's time, see Finch, *Nottingham's Chancery cases*, 73, lxx *et seq*. For a recent economic and political explanation of the rationale behind Nottingham's formulation, see G. L. Haskins, 'Extending the grasp of the dead hand: reflections on the origins of the rule against perpetuities', *University of Pennsylvania Law Review*, cxxv (1977).
114 *Mary Portington's Case* (1614), 10 Co. Rep. 35b.

considering them indestructible. Such a determination created a gap in the otherwise consistent policy of the common law courts to discourage restraints upon alienation, and highlighted the need for a uniform rule against perpetuities. While the temporary sanction of restraints upon alienation by executory devise had little effect upon marriage settlements, it did have a bearing upon the overall question of perpetuities; therefore, it may be apposite to note briefly these developments.

The first concession of the common law courts regarding the indestructibility of equitable future interests came in their treatment of executory devises of terms of years. Although a valuable interest, the common law considered the term to be a mere chattel and treated it rather harshly. However, Chancery retained control over executory interests in terms, since they had not been executed by the Statute of Uses. Perhaps out of fear that the Chancellor would intervene to protect these interests and deprive the common law courts of valuable business, the judges began to retreat from their position that executory devises of terms should be subject to the rules of destructibility of contingent remainders.[115]

Because the common law regarded an estate for life to be a greater interest than a lease of a term of years,[116] a gift of the residue of a term after a life estate was not initially recognized. However, in 1578, it was held that a gift over of a term in the form of an executory devise after the death of the life tenant was valid.[117] Thereafter, Chancery spurred the common law courts to find this interest indestructible by entertaining suits brought by the holder of the future interest to compel the tenant for life to put in security not to bar his interest. And in *Manning's Case*[118] and *Lampet's Case*[119] executory devises over after the death of the life tenant were held to

115 H. Finch, *Lord Nottingham's manual of Chancery practice and prolegomena of Chancery and Equity*, ed. D. E. C. Yale (Cambridge, 1965), 203. Cf. *H.E.L.*, VII, 130.
116 The law adhered to this presumption regardless of the length of the term. During this period, terms of 1,000 years were not uncommon. Yet Chancery was not always receptive to long terms. In 44 Eliz., a manuscript relates, 'My Lord Keeper [Ellesmere] delivered publiquely in Court that he should not relieve leases parroll nor perpetuities nor lease for 1,000 years in land holden of the Queen in Capitae, Knight Service and ordinarie socage or any other so much be it to defraud her Majesty [of revenue] . . .', *Court of Chancery*, 'Observations in course of Chancery practice', C.U.L. MS Gg. ii. 31, fos. 812–13.
117 *Weledon* v. *Elkington* (1578), Plowden 519.
118 (1609), 8 Co. Rep. 94b.
119 (1612), 10 Co. Rep. 46b.

be indestructible. Once the courts recognized the indestructibility of executory devises in terms, it did not take long for the judges to apply the same rules to freeholds; and this was done in *Pells* v. *Brown*.[120] But it is clear from the report of the case that this step was taken with great reluctance owing to the fear that settlors would use these executory interests to create perpetuities.[121]

As Professor Simpson has noted, the decisions in *Manning's Case* and *Lampet's Case*, and in *Pells* v. *Brown* marked the failure of the common law courts to control settlors who employed uses by subjecting them to the common law rules of destructibility.[122] With regard to both leaseholds and freeholds, future interests in the form of executory devises taking effect under the Statute of Wills were not considered to be governed by the rules of destructibility of contingent remainders. In addition, active trusts were not within the ambit of the Statute of Uses, and were not confined by any rules. Thus the only meagre protection against the creation of perpetuities was the rule that any future interest which could be regarded as a contingent remainder must be so regarded;[123] it now became evident that unless some checks were placed upon the power of disposition by way of use, settlors would be free to manipulate executory interests to create perpetuities.

Having allowed the creation of a gift over of a term after life estate in a term, the court resolved to go no further. Whether a gift over could follow an entail came before the court in *Childe* v. *Baille*,[124] where a term had been devised 'to A and his heirs, but if A died without issue then the term was to go to B'. The court construed this to be an entail, and an unbarrable one at that, since the termor would be unable to create a tenant to the *praecipe* against whom a recovery could be brought. So the court held the gift of the entail void, and determined that the conveyance operated as an outright grant of the term. Thus the common law rule on executory devises

---

120 (1620), Cro. Jac. 590. Yet *Pells* v. *Brown* is not as anomalous a decision as some legal historians have suggested. The devise was 'to younger son but if he dies without issue in the lifetime of his elder brother, then to eldest son'. In substance this grant was similar to the alternative contingent interest sanctioned in *Colethirst* v. *Bejushin*, see above, pp. 28–31.

121 Justice Doderidge argued that a recovery should bar the gift over: 'For otherwise it would be a mischievious kind of perpetuity which could not by any means be destroyed': (1620), Cro. Jac. 590, 592.

122 Simpson, *Land law*, 208–9.

123 Set forth in *Purefoy* v. *Rodgers* (1669), 2 Wm Saunders 380, 398, but recognized in *Chudleigh's Case* (1595), 1 Co. Rep. 130a.

124 (1618), Cro. Jac. 459, confirmed in *Saunders* v. *Cornish* (1639), Cro. Car. 230.

in leaseholds was this: the limitation of a gift over was good if it followed a life estate, but void if it followed a greater interest.[125] Since in *Pells* the executory limitation had followed a fee simple, this decision shattered the uniformity in the treatment of executory devises in both leaseholds and freeholds without offering much in the way of protection against perpetuities. Indeed the gift over after the entail in *Childe* v. *Baille* was no more remote than the one following the life estate in *Manning's Case*, since it had to vest or fail at the death of A. Counsel vainly pursued this point, arguing that there was no more danger of a perpetuity in this interest than in a common law life estate.[126] Although the argument proved unsuccessful, it did suggest that, in determining whether a settlement should be upheld, the focus should be upon remoteness of vesting rather than upon the form of the conveyance, a view which eventually prevailed.[127]

While the altered posture of the common law courts towards the indestructibility of executory devises allowed the landowner a greater degree of flexibility in the disposition of his estate, these developments had little bearing upon the legal form of marriage settlements, since they only applied to dispositions by will. During the latter half of the sixteenth century, those settlors bent upon creating perpetuities in marriage settlements could experiment only with the creation of executory interests in freeholds. Such settlements took the form of either 'unbarrable entails' or 'perpetual freeholds', and the more daring amongst conveyancers and their clients dabbled in them. But it was hardly likely that the common law courts would sanction these devices, struggling as they were with future interests which only *might* be employed to create perpetuities. That these clauses were invented and employed in settlements testifies both to the ingenuity of the conveyancers and to the overwhelming desire of some landowners to restrain alienation in perpetuity.[128]

---

125 Chancery likewise refused to recognize a gift over after the entail of trust in a term of years: *Tatton* v. *Molineux* (1611), Pollex. 24; *Ireland* v. *Payne* (1638), Pollex. 25.

126 (1618), Cro. Jac. 459, 460.

127 In the *Duke of Norfolk's Case* (1681), 3 Ch. Cas. 1.

128 It must, however, be conceded that the extent of the use of perpetuities has never been demonstrated by even as unsophisticated a quantitative method as I shall be employing both to establish the prevailing mode of settlement in the first half of the seventeenth century and to gauge the adoption of the strict settlement.

One of the most curious attempts to create an unbarrable entail comes to light in *Wiseman's Case*.[129] In a settlement of 1582, an attempt was made to use a statute[130] which prevented an estate tail granted by the Crown from being barred so long as the Crown retained a remainder or reversionary interest. The form employed was this: 'tenant in fee covenants to stand seised to the use of himself in tail, and then to the use of his brother in tail, remainder to the use of the Queen in fee'. Tenant in tail suffered a common recovery and died without issue; did the recovery bar the remainders, since the ultimate remainder in fee was in the Queen? After finding that no valuable consideration had passed from the Queen to raise a use in her, the court went on to hold that the statute applied only to entails created by the Crown, or where the Crown had procured an entail from a subject limited to a third person with a remainder in the Crown. Thus this rather ingenious attempt to restrain alienation was to no avail.

Generally, the methods which settlors adopted to create unbarrable entails were more direct. In *Scholastica's Case*,[131] a landowner had devised estates to his wife for life with successive remainders in tail to his elder son, his younger son and his daughter. Included within the will was a provision that if any of the devisees alienated or mortgaged the lands, the estates should 'descend and come unto the party next in tail unto him or them, as effectively as if such disorderous person or persons had never been minded of in this my present testament and last will'.[132] The proviso was held to be a limitation rather than a condition, and it was adjudged valid. It would appear that the court was willing to countenance flexibility in devises; Plowden noted a statement by Dyer: 'For in a man's last will he has power like unto an Act of Parliament . . . so that the law submits itself to the manner, order and form limited in last wills, and requires that the same shall be observed.'[133] Although Coke denied that the case was resolved in favour of the limitation, it would appear that he was merely justifying a reversal of doctrine.[134] Moreover, in *Rudhall* v. *Milwards* a similar clause was held valid.[135]

129 (1585), 2 Co. Rep. 10b.
130 34 Hen. VII c. 20.
131 (1572), Plowden 408. The will was executed in 1557.
132 *Ibid.*, 409.
133 *Ibid.*, 413.
134 *Mary Portington's Case* (1614), 10 Co. Rep. 35b, 47a.
135 (1586), Moo. K.B. 212. The report does not give the date of the devise.

There is, however, some evidence in addition to Coke's justification which suggests that the decision in *Scholastica's Case* was an aberration. As early as 1550, Chief Justice Mountague had suggested that such limitations were repugnant to the nature of an estate tail.[136] It is not unlikely that the limitation was considered valid because it was created by will, since the courts were more lenient in their treatment of executory devises. Regardless, the decision was short-lived, with outright reversal of the position in *Mary Portington's Case*. Moreover, the decision in *Scholastica's Case* was never extended to *inter vivos* settlements. In *Corbet's Case*[137] a father covenanted to stand seised to the use of his sons for life with remainders in tail to his successive younger sons:

and it was provided, covenanted, and agreed by the same indenture . . . that if the said R and etc. one of the younger sons or any of his heirs male of his body should be resolved or determined or advisedly should attempt, or promise an act or thing concerning an alienation of or for the said manor, etc. by which the estate tail thereof before limited should be undone, barred or determined, or by which the same should not come, remain and be in manner and form as limited by the same indenture; after that, and before such act done, by which etc., before any such bargain, discontinuance etc. had or executed etc. should cease only in respect and having regard to such persons so attempting in the same manner, quality, degree, and condition as if such person so attempting was naturally dead and not otherwise . . .[138]

Here the court held the condition, which created a perpetuity, void.

Although the underlying legal rationale for defeating this attempt to produce a forfeiture if the tenant in tail attempted to bar the entail was that the ability to alienate by common recovery was intrinsic to the nature of an estate tail, the court provided a series of 'repugnancies' which would be most satisfying to the contemporary lawyer. First, it was repugnant to the law that a condition should defeat part of the estate tail, but still allow the rest to take effect; or as it was stated quite simply, an estate cannot cease if it continues. Secondly, the proviso was repugnant to the nature of an estate tail because such an estate can determine only upon death without issue, so the death of the tenant in tail alone could not affect the estate. Finally, it was a 'manifest repugnancy' that by the first part of the proviso the estate should not cease until an attempt to

136 (1550), Plowden 21, 34.
137 (1599), 1 Co. Rep. 84a. The report does not give the date of the settlement; it may well be a feigned case.
138 *Ibid.*, 84b.

alienate was accomplished, and by the second part of the proviso the estate should cease upon an attempt to alienate, but before actual accomplishment. Thus the attempt to create a perpetuity by shifting possession to the next heir should the tenant in possession alienate failed.

Substantially similar settlements had come before the court in two other cases cited in the report.[139] Moreover, it is important to note that in *Mildmay's Case*[140] the judges began to discuss practical policy considerations with regard to perpetuities, as well as the doctrinal difficulties which the settlement engendered. For example, it was argued that to forfeit an interest on a mere attempt to alienate would make titles too uncertain, since one could never be sure what constituted an attempt. Moreover, the reporter related that the judges announced that perpetuities were against the reason and policy of the law; it was considered that: 'Lastly the intent of the statute of 27 Henry VIII was to restore the ancient common law and to root out all subtile inventions, imaginations and practice of uses which had introduced many mischiefs and inconveniences mentioned in the preamble.'[141]

Consequently, when the devise in *Mary Portington's Case*[142] came before the court, the judges avoided discussion of the legal repugnancies discussed in *Corbet's Case*; it was simply held that no condition or limitation was valid if it attempted to restrain a tenant in tail from suffering a recovery.[143] By so holding, the court disallowed a proviso similar to one it had previously sanctioned in *Scholastica's Case* where the restraint was construed to be a limitation rather than a condition.[144] But by this time it was clear that any attempt to create an unbarrable entail by any means would fail, and that the judges were willing to strike down perpetuities without searching for 'repugnancies'. As Coke commented: 'it was observed that these perpetuities were born under some unfortunate constellation'.[145]

---

139 *Ascot* v. *Cermin* and *Cholmley* v. *Humble*, discussed in 1 Co. Rep. 84a, 85a–86a.
140 (1606), 6 Co. Rep. 40a.
141 *Ibid.*, 43a.
142 (1614), 10 Co. Rep. 35b. The will was executed in 1582.
143 By providing that upon the execution of any act which prevented the estate from descending as directed by the settlor then the estate of the person should cease as if he died without heirs of the body.
144 (1572), Plowden 408.
145 (1614), 10 Co. Rep. 35b, 42b.

The other device contrived to create perpetuities by the use of executory interests in freeholds was a form of limitation known as a 'perpetual freehold'. The legal form of this device was as follows: 'to the use of A for life, remainder to the use of A's son for life, remainder to the use of that son's son and so on *ad infinitum*'. Such a limitation on its face was only a series of valid contingent uses which were safe from destruction; but, if upheld, the limitation would in effect create a perpetuity, since each tenant would have only an estate for life and never an alienable fee.[146] Recognizing this, the court in *Lovelace* v. *Lovelace*[147] held that only remainders vesting before the determination of the first life estate were valid, since it was the one which supported *all* the remainders.

So by the second decade of the seventeenth century the judicial exclusion of the unbarrable entail and the perpetual freehold, coupled with the treatment of contingent remainders at common law, left only executory devises in freeholds as vehicles to create perpetuities. Although this interest might be employed to facilitate the hereditary disposition of estates, executory devises were of no use in the formulation of marriage settlements. Furthermore, with the hostility of the judges to lengthy settlements so apparent, it is likely that many conveyancers were cautious even in employing these interests.[148] Indeed, by 1623, a manual outlining Chancery practice concluded: 'All suits grounded . . . for the establishment of the Perpetuities . . . are regularly to be dismissed upon motion if they be the whole matter of the Bill . . .'[149] And, in his compendium of the laws of England, William Sheppard noted: 'But being found of dangerous consequence, the Law hath adjudged all these Conditions against Law and so void, and by this avoided Perpetuities.'[150]

Thus by the early seventeenth century, with a few notable exceptions regarding executory devises, the policy of the common law courts toward restraints upon alienation was decidedly hostile.

146 Therefore, the tenant in possession could not suffer a common recovery.
147 Cited in *Perrot's Case* (1576), Moo. K.B. 368, 371.
148 Holdsworth, commenting upon the proposed statute of 1598 to abolish perpetuities (which for unknown reasons never became law), considered that the courts 'were then fully resolved as they always have been resolved both before and since to stamp out these perpetuities': *H.E.L.*, VII, 214.
149 Thomas Powell, *The attorney's academy* (London, 1623), 45–6.
150 William Sheppard, *An epitome of all the common and statute laws of the nation* (London, 1656), 796.

Even before *Corbet's Case* (1599), the discussion of executory interests in *Chudleigh's Case* (1595) forewarned the profession that such attempts were in disfavour; it is not unlikely that the case formed the doctrinal basis for the reversal on perpetuities embodied in the decision in *Mary Portington's Case* (1614). Points of uncertainty were relatively few, and what was perhaps more important to the landowner was that secure alternatives to these legally questionable forms were being sanctioned. Before describing the mechanics employed in these alternative settlements, it may be appropriate to consider the effect of the judicial policy on the question of perpetuities.

It seems clear that the reversal on the issue of perpetuities had no unsettling effect upon inheritances. The invalidity of the gift over in effect merely rendered the present tenant in possession by force of the perpetuity seised of an entail with the ability to bar the interest. Although the policy may have confounded the designs of those landowners who employed perpetuities, it did not result in the dispossession of tenants. Perhaps the most significant effect was that it allowed the alienation of estates which would otherwise have been excluded from the land market.

In considering the impact of *Mary Portington's Case*, it must be appreciated that the extent of the employment of perpetuities has never been established. It is likely that practitioners quickly abandoned them in spite of their appearance in subsequent conveyancing books.[151] It has been argued that disputes in certain inheritances were engendered by uncertainty in the law regarding perpetuities.[152] Without considering these controversies in depth here,[153] it is enough to note that legal wranglings over inheritances were not peculiar to this period, particularly where there was no

151 Printed conveyancing books continued to reproduce perpetuities after 1614. See for example, John Herne, *The modern assurancer: or the clerk's directory* (London, 1658), 128. J. P. Cooper noted similar precedents in West's *Symbolaeographia*: Cooper, 'Patterns of inheritance', 20, fn. 55. But it appears likely that practitioners kept their own notebooks up to date. A manuscript precedent book in the British Library has a marginal note concluding that the marriage settlement on the page contains an invalid clause of perpetuity: B.L., Add. MS 36077, fos. 16, 23–6.

152 B. Coward, 'Disputed inheritances: some problems of the nobility in the sixteenth and early seventeenth centuries', *B.I.H.R.*, XLIV (1971).

153 I have considered the disputes in depth in L. Bonfield, 'Marriage settlements 1601–1740: the development and adoption of the strict settlement' (Unpublished University of Cambridge Ph.D. thesis, 1978), 106–19.

lineal male heir. Conflicts between the collateral male heir and the heir general were not uncommon in medieval England, and they can also be observed in the late seventeenth and eighteenth centuries, periods of more settled land law.[154] In order to attribute such controversies to vagaries of the law, the cases would necessarily have involved disputes over the legal mechanics employed. In these lawsuits, this was not so; the gravamen of each dispute touched issues of fact such as birth, marriage or death, or whether the land was entailed. When one examines these controversies, they appear to deal principally with evidence and proof, and in particular with documentary uncertainties, rather than with vagaries of the law with respect to perpetuities.

The developments in doctrine outlined in this chapter were not dispositive of all or even most of the legal issues regarding the suspension of powers of alienation in settlements. Yet the common law courts had finally taken a critical step towards establishing a policy: land could not be rendered permanently inalienable, and any attempt to do so would be struck down regardless of the legal mechanics employed. At least in the negative, that is to say what could not be accomplished by a landowner, the outer limits of control by the 'dead hand' were established. A major step had been taken along the tortuous path to a comprehensive rule against perpetuities.

It would take more than a century for such a rule to be established. In the interim, there were generations of landowners with ambitions to satisfy. An ingenious segment of the legal profession which engaged in conveyancing, and it must be conceded that those men of law who drafted the devises and settlements in the cases discussed in this chapter did not lack imagination, was required to find alternatives to the unbarrable entail and the perpetuity. Perhaps guided by some of the cases highlighted above, they began to employ contingent remainders in marriage settlements. It is to this matter that we may now turn.

---

154 McFarlane, *Nobility of later medieval England*, 73–4; R. A. Kelch, *Newcastle: a duke without money* (London, 1974), 28–35. Even so prominent a legal figure as Lord Chancellor Cowper blundered, engendering a contest in Chancery over his will: Christopher Clay, 'Two families and their estates: the Grimstones and the Cowpers from *c*. 1650–*c*.1815' (Unpublished University of Cambridge Ph.D. thesis, 1966), 190–2.

3

PATTERNS OF MARRIAGE SETTLEMENT 1601–1659: THE DEVELOPMENT OF THE 'LIFE ESTATE-ENTAIL' MODE

Developments in legal doctrine are not necessarily linear. The law regarding restraints upon alienation remained sufficiently hazy to be malleable. Moreover, the commitment of the common law judges to free alienability need not have been irreversible; after all, the period separating *Scholastica's Case* and *Mary Portington's Case* was little more than a generation.[1] Further developments in the law would depend upon the activities of lawyers engaged in conveyancing and upon the requirements of their clients, since the settlements they drafted would be the ones which came before the courts. Their reaction to the elaboration of doctrine considered in the last chapter would therefore be crucial. Would they attempt to devise even more ingenious forms of restraint; or would they fashion settlements within the bounds accepted in the cases? The purpose of this chapter is to provide an answer to this question with the best evidence available to the legal historian: the settlements themselves.

The settlements under consideration are those executed in the first sixty years of the century which are preserved in the county archives of Kent and Northamptonshire. While recognizing the limitations of the data set, it can be relied upon to support the position that by the turn of the seventeenth century conveyancers had abandoned the perpetuity in marriage settlements and employed instead permissible contingent remainders.[2] The manner in which each altered thread of legal doctrine regarding contingent remainders was manipulated to satisfy the demands of clients will be illustrated and the appearance of each mode of disposition will be tabulated.

The data suggest that the most prevalent form of marriage settlement after 1600 in Kent and Northamptonshire was a life estate in the groom followed by a jointure provision with the entail

1 1572 to 1614.
2 See Introduction.

secured in the eldest son to be produced by the union.[3] This entail, however, was contingent and therefore precarious, because it could be destroyed by the life tenant in possession even after a son was born. Thus the patrimony was not protected from a profligate squire. All the settlement did was insure the appropriate descent of estates in the possession of the life tenant at his death. Once this form was established, conveyancers devised a method of protecting the entail, and the strict settlement was spawned.

The acceptance of alternative contingent remainders to living persons in *Colethirst* v. *Bejushin* marked the first major concession on the part of the common law courts towards facilitating the employment of contingent remainders to effect more flexible marriage settlements. Of the eighty-four pre-1660 marriage settlements which comprise the data set,[4] alternative contingent remainders appear in fifteen (17.9%) of the dispositions.[5] In the main, they were employed to achieve two distinct ends. First, alternative contingent remainders were implemented much as they were in *Colethirst*, to effect a gift over of an interest to a living person upon the death of the first taker should specific conditions prevail. Secondly, this type of interest was employed in various jointure provisions to secure the widow's maintenance, following either a joint life interest to the groom and his father, or a life estate in the groom's father for the life of the groom.

Turning now to this first type of alternative contingent remainder which appears in six of the settlements,[6] a gift over to a living person in each case was directed upon the occurrence of a contingency, the death of the first taker without male issue. The general form employed ran as follows: 'to groom in tail male, (or in tail male special) but if the groom dies without issue male, then to his younger brother in tail' (who was specifically named). By employing alternative contingent remainders in this fashion, the mode of descent mandated by the laws of intestate succession might be altered. For example, in a settlement executed upon the marriage in 1602 of his heir male, Nicholas, with Francis, daughter of the Earl of Exeter, Sir John Tufton of Hothfield, Baronet, limited a life

---

3 For convenience, I shall hereinafter refer to this mode as the 'life estate-entail' form.
4 Sequence nos. 1–45, 210–39.
5 Sequence nos. 1, 3, 5, 6, 10, 14, 20, 23, 25, 26, 35, 39, 206, 215, 224.
6 Sequence nos. 1, 3, 10, 25, 35, 39.

estate to his own use in part of the patrimony if Nicholas predeceased him without leaving male issue.[7] Further, he provided a contingent remainder to his five named daughters if both Nicholas and his younger brother died without male heirs, thus depriving the collateral heir male of a considerable portion of the patrimony. In this manner, a settlor might also disinherit a younger son in favour of a collateral heir if he felt so inclined.[8]

Thus, by employing alternative contingent remainders, a landowner might mandate the ultimate disposition of his estates in the generation after his death should his eldest son die without male issue. So long as the alternate taker was alive at the time of execution of the marriage settlement, the rule elaborated in *Colethirst* gave recognition to the gift over. In addition, alternative contingent remainders were suitable in arranging more flexible jointure provisions. By their employment a settlor might secure a present interest in himself (in such a case he was generally the father of the groom) which determined upon the death of the husband, and was followed by a remainder for the life of the widow to comprise her jointure.[9] In form the disposition ran as follows: 'life estate to father for the life of the groom, if the groom survives his father life estate to the groom, but if the groom predeceases his father to bride as jointure'. Alternatively a joint life estate might be limited 'to father and groom for joint lives remainder to groom if he survives father, but to bride if groom predeceases father'.[10] By effecting such a disposition upon the marriage of his eldest son, the settlor retained the beneficial enjoyment of that segment of the patrimony which was appropriated as the bride's jointure under the settlement. Should the bride predecease the groom, the estate would devolve upon his death to whomever he named in the settlement.

Apart from employing alternative contingent remainders, the settlor might manipulate the interest in a different manner to achieve another objective. Thus in one of the marriage settlements[11] a settlor limited a life interest in himself following an initial life interest in the groom and an estate of jointure in the bride, but preceding the ultimate remainder in tail to their heir male. Such a

---

7 Sequence no. 1.
8 *Ibid.*
9 Sequence nos. 6, 23, 206, 215, 224.
10 Sequence nos. 5, 20.
11 Sequence no. 26.

disposition may have been intended to foil an attempt by the groom to bar the entail so long as the father remained alive; should his son predecease him, the settlor may have desired to receive the profits in an informal trust for the benefit of the ultimate remainderman, his grandson. Finally, he may have desired to appropriate the profits of this segment of the patrimony to his own use for the remainder of his life if he survived his son.

Such enquiry into the settlor's motives in this particular disposition must be considered sheer speculation; however, as these examples attest, the admission of alternative contingent remainders by the common law courts broadened the patterns of disposition at the disposal of the settlor. As we have seen, nearly one settlement in six employed this device. Yet it was the second thread of development in legal doctrine with regard to contingent remainders, that children not *in esse* at the time the settlement was executed might take by way of remainder if they were in being when the supporting estate determined, which produced the prevailing mode of settlement in the first sixty years of the seventeenth century. This form, 'life estate to groom, remainder to bride for life as jointure, remainder in tail to the heirs male of their bodies', was, with various modifications, employed in sixty-four of the eighty-four (76.2%) marriage settlements in the data set.[12]

Essentially this mode of marriage settlement accomplished three objectives. First, it provided maintenance for the groom's household; if either of his parents were alive the groom would not be in possession of the entire patrimony, and the income from the portion settled to his use immediately for life must have been calculated to support his family. Secondly, if the settlement was pre-nuptial it had the effect of immutably fixing the bride's jointure; but if it was executed after marriage then the provision for jointure was precatory rather than binding.[13] Finally, the entail was settled in the heir male produced by the marriage with the hope, rather than the assurance, that it would descend unimpinged.

The variations on this theme related in the main to provisions for

12 Sequence nos. 1, 2, 3, 4, 5, 7, 8, 9, 10, 11, 13, 14, 15, 17, 18, 19, 22, 23, 25, 26, 27, 30, 32, 34, 35, 36, 39, 42, 43, 44, 45, 202, 203, 205, 206, 207, 209, 210, 211, 213, 215, 216, 217, 218, 219, 220, 221, 222, 224, 225, 226, 227, 228, 229, 230, 231, 232, 233, 234, 235, 236, 237, 238, 239. Or in an alternative form: 'joint life estate to bride and groom, remainder in tail to the heirs male of their body'.
13 *Co. Litt.*, 223b.

other family members *in esse* at the time of the settlement, and to remainders over should the marriage produce no male heir. For example, the settlor might retain a life interest in himself, possibly followed by a jointure for his own wife out of part of the patrimony, while granting the remainder after his wife's death to the groom, either in tail, or for the groom's life with remainder in tail male.[14] Indeed, this was often the case in resettlements with each household enjoying the income from a portion of the estate.

Either by employing alternative contingent remainders in the manner described above or by limiting diverse remainders over, the settlor might prescribe a series of remaindermen to take in succession should no member of the previous class be ascertainable upon the determination of the preceding estate. In this manner, the fourth Lord Teynham, in a marriage settlement of 1642,[15] limited entails to his ultimate heir male, should no male heir be produced by his marriage, and in default to those of his four younger brothers successively, with remainder to the heirs male of his uncle. Indeed, some settlors used this form to disinherit the collateral heir male by limiting the remainder to female children in default of male issue.[16]

One great disadvantage to the life-entail mode of settlement was that, apart from the possible destruction of the entail, the disposition was rather rigid. With the mortgage market in its infancy, and given the limited powers to mortgage which a life tenant possessed, the tenant in possession had little alternative short of breaking the settlement to meet emergencies save by personal bond which was the most expensive way to borrow.[17] To infuse some degree of flexibility into this form of settlement, and perhaps to discourage a complete disentailing, landowners often granted their successors the freedom to dispose of a portion of the patrimony by settling a parcel in fee simple or fee tail. Of the sixty-four settlements employing the restrictive life estate-entail mode, sixteen (25%) contain partial dispositions in fee or fee tail.[18]

Clearly the emergence of the life estate-entail form as the

14 Sequence nos. 1, 4, 5, 14, 15, 17, 22, 23, 26, 27, 39, 201, 215, 216, 220, 221, 222, 225, 228, 233. In sequence nos. 1, 22, 39, 201, 220, 221, 222, 223 there were jointure provisions for the groom's mother.
15 Sequence no. 35.
16 Sequence nos. 4, 9, 17, 21, 216, 220.
17 G. E. Mingay, *English landed society in the eighteenth century* (London, 1963), 36–7.
18 Sequence nos. 1, 3, 4, 14, 15, 19, 25, 32, 35, 206, 209, 215, 218, 219, 228, 235.

prevailing mode of marriage settlement during the period was directly linked with another development mitigating the harshness of the rules of destructibility of contingent remainders. In addition to recognizing entails in unborn persons if they were ascertainable at the time at which the supporting estate determined, the modification of the rule in *Shelley's Case*[19] by the common law courts enabled the life estate-entail form to be employed in prenuptial marriage settlements. Enunciated in 1579 but apparently established by the mid-fourteenth century,[20] the rule considered a grant 'to A for life, remainder to the heirs male of his body' to convey an entail to A rather than a gift of two separate legal interests, a life estate in A and an entail in his heirs. Consequently, a groom under such a marriage settlement obtained a barrable interest which remained so even after the birth of a male heir, despite the apparent contrary intent of the settlor. When the court in *Lewis Bowles's Case*[21] modified the rule by recognizing that such a disposition created two separate interests, a life estate in the groom and an entail in his heirs, life estate-entail marriage settlements were far more secure. The descent of the reversion no longer defeated the contingent remainder in the unborn male heir. In our data set, the relaxation of the rule in *Shelley's Case* protected forty-five of the sixty-four (70.3%) life estate-entail settlements.[22]

But the protection of the entail afforded by these rulings was somewhat limited. As has been noted, the most significant disadvantage of the life estate-entail form of settlement was that the entail was contingent until the death of the life tenant. This was the case because the entail was limited to the heir male produced by the marriage. If one's heirs could only be determined at death, then the remainder was limited to an unascertained person until that time, and as such was contingent. Thus it could be destroyed by an alienation on the part of the life tenant. Some evidence exists to suggest that the profession was at work to devise a form which would render the settlement vulnerable for a shorter period. The method adopted was to limit entails successively to the first, second

19 (1579), 1 Co. Rep. 93b.
20 Simpson, *Land law*, 91.
21 (1612), 11 Co. Rep. 79b.
22 Sequence nos 1, 4, 5, 8, 14, 15, 17, 19, 22, 23, 24, 26, 27, 30, 36, 39, 201, 202, 205, 207, 209, 210, 211, 212, 213, 217, 218, 219, 220, 221, 222, 224, 225, 226, 227, 228, 229, 230, 233, 234, 235, 236, 237, 238, 239.

EDINBURGH UNIVERSITY LIBRARY
WITHDRAWN

and third son produced by the marriage.[23] Each son would be ascertained at birth, and arguably the remainder vested at that time.
Accordingly, in settlements limiting the entail in this manner, the
life tenant could defeat the interest of the contingent remaindermen
only until the birth of his first male child. If the eldest son died, not
an uncommon occurrence in the period, the entail vested in the next
living son. The entail could only be defeated by a life tenant without
a living son.

Thus our data suggest that the life estate-entail settlement had
come to be the prevailing form of marriage settlement in Kent and
Northamptonshire during the first half of the seventeenth century.
Some contemporary comment may be offered to confirm that the
use of this type of disposition was sufficiently widespread to spark
controversy regarding abuses inherent in the form of settlement.
William Sheppard, for example, in enumerating provisions in the
law which were 'said to be somewhat unreasonable and fit to be
changed', included the following: 'That a man may have an Estate
at his disposal, and yet not lyable to his debts, as . . . an Estate of life
to the Father, the Remainder to his Eldest son, before he hath a
son . . .'.[24] In addition to settling the patrimony, the form had this
further 'inconvenient' advantage.

In illustrating the emerging form of marriage settlement which
was fostered by the concessions of the common law courts outlined
above, the precarious nature of the settlement has been emphasized.
There was, however, a form of settlement which might offer further
protection. By taking a life interest in a portion of the estate which
he settled upon his eldest son, the landowner not only secured
maintenance for himself, but also 'bought time'; for if he survived
his son the entail was secured.

Yet the patterns of marriage settlements which emerge from the
analysis of the legal forms employed in the data set tend to indicate
that restraining one's heirs from alienating the patrimony may not
have been a paramount goal of landowners. For example, in ten[25] of

23 Although limitations in this manner appear in only one settlement in the data set
    (sequence no. 11), manuscript conveyancing books provide examples of the
    mechanics by the close of the sixteenth century. B.L., Add. MS 36077, fos.
    18–22, 23–6, 26–8, 30–4, 36–45; C.U.L. MS Dd. ii. 46, fos. 55–8; C.U.L. MS Ee.
    i. 6, fos. 22–9. A 1646 settlement preserved in a manuscript conveyancing book
    refers to their manner of limitation 'as in ordinary conveyances': B.L., Harleian
    MS 2053, fos. 15–16.
24 William Sheppard, *England's balme* (London, 1657), 211, 214.
25 Sequence nos. 6, 13, 16, 20, 24, 28, 29, 201, 212, 214.

the eighty-four settlements (11.9%), fee simple interests were granted to the groom: five[26] were granted outright, while the other five[27] followed life estates limited to the settlor. Despite the implementation of fifteen post-nuptial settlements,[28] no settlor appears to have delayed execution until the birth of a male grandson so as to limit a life interest in him, thereby preventing his son from alienating the patrimony.[29]

Moreover, another variation of the life estate-entail form which was the most likely to secure the entire patrimony in the settlor's grandson if he survived his son, whilst at the same time both providing for the present maintenance of the groom's household and fixing the widow's jointure, was employed only once.[30] The settlement ran as follows: 'life estate to father, subject to an annuity of £300 in favour of groom and bride and the survivor in lieu of jointure, remainder to groom for life, remainder to bride as jointure, remainder in tail male'. John Raynes, Esquire, employed this form in 1624, one which accomplished all three major goals of the marriage settlement; and if he survived his son the settlement secured the passage of the entire patrimony to the grandson intact. Although a gamble at best, this form was clearly the most effective means to bridle one's heir, yet it was employed in only one marriage settlement in the data set.

Thus one might conclude from this enquiry into the forms of marriage settlement executed in Kent and Northamptonshire from 1600 to 1659 that settlors in the main did not avail themselves of the most effective means of fettering their estate, and that the concern of landowners with restraints upon alienation would appear to be less compelling, at least after 1600, than some historians have suggested. The life estate-entail pattern did satisfy the need of landowners: maintenance for the new family was assured, jointure was fixed, and descent of the patrimony was directed. The major shortcoming was the risk that the groom would alienate. During the 1640s, two settlements appear in which trusts were limited during the life of the groom.[31] Although the clauses do not specify that the

26 Sequence nos. 6, 13, 24, 212, 214.
27 Sequence nos. 16, 20, 28, 29, 201.
28 Sequence nos. 5, 10, 11, 12, 23, 26, 27, 201, 204, 205, 209, 216, 220, 228, 230.
29 The manner of settlement employed by John Isham in Finch, *Northamptonshire families*, 23.
30 Sequence no. 19.
31 Sequence nos. 229, 234.

limitation in trust was to preserve the contingent entail, the similarity in form suggests that these are rudimentary strict settlements. Having established the prevailing form of settlement in the early seventeenth century, we may now investigate its protective modification.

4

THE EMERGENCE OF THE STRICT
SETTLEMENT

In the preceding chapter, the manner in which the alteration in the attitude of the common law courts towards the manipulation of contingent remainders facilitated the emergence of the life estate-entail form of marriage settlement during the first half of the seventeenth century has been demonstrated. At the same time, however, the precarious nature of the entail which this mode of settlement conferred upon the eldest son produced by the marriage has been noted. Under the rules of destructibility of contingent remainders, a complex body of law established to ensure that these future interests were not employed to create long-term restraints upon alienation, a forfeiture or tortious feoffment by the life tenant in possession would defeat the contingent entail settled upon the male heir produced by the marriage.[1] Essentially, then, what the common law courts had sanctioned was the transfer of the patrimony from one generation to the next by marriage settlement; but they had adamantly refused to restrain the freedom of disposition of the tenant in possession to insure that the entail descended unimpinged to the next generation. Around the middle of the seventeenth century, conveyancers developed a device by which they sought to secure this entail in the male heir – the trust to preserve contingent remainders. In this chapter, the origins of the device will be traced, and the elaboration of legal doctrine regarding the nature of the innovation in the courts of common law and equity will be considered.

The mechanics employed by conveyancers to secure the entail were indeed quite simple. A limitation to trustees was inserted after

---

1 If the supporting estate determined before the contingent limitation was to take effect, there would be an abeyance of seisin; and thus the remainder would be destroyed.

the life estate in the groom, but preceding the entail in the unborn male heir:

And from and after the determination of that Estate [the life estate in the groom], To the use and behoof of H. K. of the Inner Temple, Gent., his heirs and Assigns, for and during the natural life of the said W. P. [the life tenant] upon Trust only, for preserving the contingent Uses and Estates herein after limited, and to make Entries for the same, if it shall be needful . . .[2]

Thus if for any reason the life estate in the groom were to determine prematurely (i.e. before his natural death), thereby terminating the estate of freehold which supported the contingent entail, the trust came into operation to secure the contingent remainder from destruction. The use of the trust in this fashion insured that the entail was no longer at the mercy of the life tenant in possession.

Whether the trust functioned in this protective manner, however, depended upon the construction which the courts placed upon the quality of estate in the trustees, and how they undertook to protect the interest of the contingent remainderman. In the first place, it was essential for the judges to construe the estate in the trustees to be vested; for if their interest was considered contingent, the estate in the trustees would be destroyed by those very same acts of the life tenant from which it sought to protect the entail. Put simply, a limitation in trustees which was considered contingent rather than vested could not protect the entail, because it would likewise be destroyed by an alienation. The second question raised by the trust dealt with remedies. Assuming the limitation as vested, it was necessary for the courts to impose a duty upon the trustees to intercede where the life tenant attempted to defeat the entail. If they failed to act, it was necessary for the courts to provide a retrospective remedy for breach of trust.

For very different reasons both these issues were quite thorny. With regard to the quality of estate in the trustees, it appears that according to accepted legal doctrine the limitation in the trustees was indeed contingent. In defining contingent remainders, Charles Fearne concluded that 'we may properly distinguish four sorts of contingent remainders. First, where the remainder depends entirely upon a contingent determination of the preceding estate

---

2 *Bridgeman's conveyances*, 2nd edn (London, 1690), 93. The precise wording of the limitations varied slightly from settlement to settlement.

itself.'[3] According to the terms of the trust, it is clear that the trustees would come into possession of their interest only if the precedent estate determined prematurely. This event was, of course, uncertain, because the life tenant might not seek to destroy the entail. Moreover, the other occurrence which brought the trust into operation, a forfeiture, was likewise an uncertain event. With regard to remedies against the trustees for nonfeasance, the problem was practical rather than doctrinal. Since the role of the trustees was to protect the contingent entail settled in the male heir, there was no aggrieved party *in esse* to sue for specific performance at the precise moment when the life estate prematurely determined, the event which required the trust to come into operation to support the contingent remainder. In cases of forfeiture, the next vested remainderman would immediately come into possession if the trustees did not perform their duties under the settlement. However, the primary purpose of the trust was to prevent the life tenant from unilaterally destroying the contingent entail by levying a fine or suffering a recovery. Where the trustees failed to intercede to prevent the disposition of settled estates, valuable consideration would likely have passed from the vendee. What was the appropriate remedy, and against whom did it lie?

During the second half of the seventeenth century and the first part of the eighteenth, the courts of common law and Chancery grappled with these two problems. In the end, the common law courts held the remainder to be vested by re-defining the distinction between vested and contingent remainders.[4] In part, this alteration was undertaken because of collateral developments in Chancery regarding perpetuities; as we have seen, one of the paramount reasons for construing remainders to be contingent was to thwart their use in creating settlements which circumscribed powers of alienation by subjecting them to the rules of destructibility. During this same period, the first steps were taken to devise a uniform rule against perpetuities, thus allaying the fears of the common law judges regarding the dangers inherent in the manipulation of contingent remainders. With the focus of the developing rule against perpetuities squarely based upon remoteness of vesting

3 Charles Fearne, *An essay on the learning of contingent remainders*, 7th edn (London, 1820), 5.
4 In *Dormer* v. *Parkhurst* (1740), 6 Bro. P.C. 351.

rather than upon legal form, the distinction between the two types of remainder was no longer so vital.

Remedies, however, were to be sought in Chancery. Before Chancery could fashion a suitable one for nonfeasance by the trustees, the Chancellor had to consider which acts or omissions constituted a breach of trust. Ultimately, he came to consider almost any complicity on the part of the trustees to constitute a breach of trust if their actions had the effect of depriving the contingent remainderman of his interest. The developments in Chancery, however, were chequered; and the period witnessed some cases in which the Chancellor compelled the trustees to join in a conveyance to destroy the settlement. However, in cases where the court found a clear breach of trust, the restoration of the estates under settlement was compelled if the purchaser had notice of the trust; if he did not, then the burden fell entirely upon the trustees, and the court required them to settle estates of similar quality upon the remainderman. The role of Chancery in determining the validity of the strict settlement was critical, because before the common law courts had occasion to define the nature of the estate in the trustees in 1697, the Chancellor had already undertaken to enforce the trust. By so doing, Chancery by implication construed the limitation in the trustees to be vested. Before tracing these separate, though interrelated, developments regarding the quality of the estate in trustees, the origins of the device may be considered.

The eighteenth-century version of the provenance of the strict settlement was concisely expressed by Blackstone:

This method is said to have been invented by Sir Orlando Bridgeman and Sir Geoffrey Palmer, and other eminent counsel who betook themselves to conveyancing during the time of the civil wars; in order thereby to secure in family settlements a provision for the future children of an intended marriage, who before were usually left at the mercy of the particular tenant for life: and when after the restoration, those gentlemen came to fill the first offices of the law, they supported this invention within reasonable and proper bounds, and introduced it into general use.[5]

It is likely that Blackstone derived his view in part from the opinion of Lord Chancellor Hardwicke in *Garth* v. *Cotton*.[6] Hardwicke believed that its introduction was connected with the civil war: 'it was not brought into practice until the time of the usurpation, when

5 2 *Bl. Comm.*, 172.
6 (1735), Dickens 183, 191.

providing against forfeitures . . . was an additional motive to it'. In addition to discussing the provenance of the strict settlement, Lord Hardwicke also elaborated upon the legal developments which required the invention of a device to protect family settlements, and speculated upon the case law which may have inspired the form which the innovation assumed. Hardwicke believed it was the intimation of the judges in *Chudleigh's Case*,[7] and their subsequent determination in *Archer's Case*,[8] that contingent uses were liable to destruction by a feoffment of the life tenant in the same manner as legal contingent remainders, which required 'chasms and defects to be supplied'.[9]

According to Lord Hardwicke the 'germ of the device' emanated from Sir Edward Coke's discussion of the validity of the settlement before the court in *Cholmley's Case*.[10] In attempting to explain the invalidity of a gift over of a remainder for the life of the tenant in tail in a conveyance of an entail, Coke argued that the remainder must be void. Such an interest, he asserted, can never take effect in possession, because an entail is not subject to a forfeiture. In contrast, Coke supplied two examples of grants of gifts over which were valid; and Lord Hardwicke considered the first to be the inspiration for the strict settlement: 'a grant of a remainder over to X for the life of Y in a conveyance of a life estate to Y is good; "for by possibility the remainder may take effect, *scil.* if the tenant for life makes a feoffment in fee or commits any forfeiture, he in remainder may enter for the forfeiture"'.[11] Yet it seems clear that this 'possibility' is a contingent interest. With the trustees to preserve contingent remainders, it is crucial that the remainder be vested for the trustees to perform their protective function.

However, it appears that it was the second example put forward by Coke, but omitted by Lord Hardwicke in his exposition, which formed the doctrinal basis for the courts' determination that the estate in the trustees was vested. The illustration provided by Coke was where a settlor limited the reversion to another during the life of

---

7 (1595), 1 Co. Rep. 120b.
8 (1597), 1 Co. Rep. 66a.
9 (1753), Dickens 183, 193.
10 (1597), 2 Co. Rep. 50a.
11 *Ibid.*, 51a. A precedent for such a clause exists in a conveyancing book of the reign of Elizabeth: B.L., Add. MS 25240, fos. 144–6. The limitation is ' to elder son for life until he attempts to alienate, remainder to the use of younger son for the life of the elder son'.

the tenant in tail; such a grant was valid because an interest immediately passed to the grantee: 'he that has the reversion shall have the services which the tenant in tail ought to do during the life of the tenant in tail'.[12] Ultimately this reasoning provided the rationale in considering the estate in the trustees to be vested; for it was considered that the vested reversion left in the settlor 'when conveyed to the trustees is a vested remainder or legal estate'.[13]

Modern historians, both legal and economic, have adopted this 'eighteenth-century tradition' on the origins of the strict settlement.[14] Moreover, the prominence of Sir Orlando Bridgeman in the development of the strict settlement has been secured by the posthumous publication of his conveyancing precedents, many of which contain examples of strict settlements.[15] But there is a dearth of substantive evidence linking Sir Orlando with the inspiration for the mechanics. Blackstone's contention that Bridgeman supported the device 'within reasonable and proper bounds'[16] finds no support in Bridgeman's manuscript notes penned during his tenure as Chief Justice of the Court of Common Pleas.[17] Moreover, reports of his decisions as Lord Keeper contain no case in which the validity of the limitation is considered.[18] Indeed, Sir Orlando did not employ the device to assure his own estate. A staunch Royalist, Bridgeman paid dearly for his loyalty; the majority of his estate was held in fee simple, and he compounded for his delinquency to the tune of £1,968 5s 9d.[19]

12 (1597), 2 Co. Rep. 50a.
13 Charles Viner, *A general abridgement of law and equity*, 2nd edn (24 vols., London, 1797), XVIII, 416.
14 *H.E.L.*, VII, 111–13; and Simpson, *Land law*, 219. H. J. Habakkuk, 'Marriage settlements in the eighteenth century', *T.R.H.S.*, 4th ser. XXXII (1950); Finch, *Northamptonshire families*, xv.
15 *Bridgeman's conveyances*, 84–8, 196–211, 221–9, 256–72, 357–69, 392–8. Precedents of settlements not employing trustees to preserve contingent remainders also appear: *ibid.*, 110–13, 128, 331–4. In an admirable piece of detective work, Professor Habakkuk has managed to identify the parties involved in two of the conveyances included in the precedent book: Habakkuk, 'Marriage settlements', 21, fn. 2.
16 2 *Bl. Comm.*, 172
17 Bridgeman's manuscript notes are in B.L., Hargrave MSS 55–8. Some of the cases were edited and printed in the nineteenth century: *Bridgeman's reports*, ed. S. Bannister (London, 1823).
18 3 Ch. Rep. 66–78.
19 S.P., *Committee for compounding*, G.3, 331; S.P., *Committee for compounding*, G.192, 457–9. For a complete account of Bridgeman's difficulties, see R. O. Bridgeman and C. O. Bridgeman, 'The sequestration papers of Sir Orlando Bridgeman', *Transactions of the Shropshire Archaeological Society*, 3rd ser. II (1902).

It may, however, be apposite to note that although Bridgeman's eldest son John was only 15 in 1646, and therefore not of marriageable age, a substantial estate which was in fact part of the Bridgeman patrimony escaped the wrath of the Committee for Compounding in Shropshire. Upon Bridgeman's marriage to Judith Kynaston in 1627, the Morton estates in Shropshire were settled to her use for life, remainder to their issue in tail. Upon her death in 1644, the estates descended to John, and as a minor his estates were not subject to sequestration.[20] Perhaps it was this good fortune which may have inspired Sir Orlando to develop a marriage settlement which placed the entail in an unborn son or a minor.

Yet, if Sir Orlando invented the mechanics of the strict settlement and advised its use to his clients,[21] it is clear that he did not employ it to settle his patrimony. In 1644, Judith Kynaston died, and four years later Bridgeman remarried Dorothy Craddock, a Staffordshire widow. Although the marriage settlement itself does not survive, the detailed Articles of Agreement are preserved amongst the Bradford muniments in Weston Park.[22] According to the Articles, Sir Orlando was to convey the manor of Wigland, a moiety of the Saltwiches in Wigland, and a moiety of Wolvesacre to John Saunders, M.D., provost of Oriel College, Oxford, who was to stand seised of the premises valued at £200 per annum to the following uses: 'to Sir Orlando for life, and then to Dorothy for life in full recompense of jointure, with remainder to the heirs male of their bodies'. No estate was limited in trustees to preserve contingent remainders to prevent Bridgeman from defeating the entail in the eldest son produced by the marriage.

While it might be argued that Bridgeman did not wish to relinquish the power of disposition over the settled estates, and therefore chose not to include a limitation to trustees to preserve contingent remainders, he did effect a resettlement of a portion of

20 Bridgeman and Bridgeman, 'Sequestration papers', 20–1.
21 The precedents which are included in *Bridgeman's conveyances* are drafts of actual settlements.
22 Sir Orlando's family papers are in the hands of the Earl of Bradford. Certain of the Bradford manuscripts are in the process of being re-catalogued by Mrs D. Randall of the Staffordshire Record Office. The reference numbers are the ones which refer to the catalogue at Weston Park. I am grateful to the Earl of Bradford for allowing the transfer of the Bridgeman collection to the Staffordshire Record Office, and I am indebted to Mrs Randall for her assistance in arranging the transfer. Bradford Papers, Weston Park, Class 5/7: Articles of Agreement, 16 April 1647.

the patrimony upon the marriage of his eldest son, John, with Mary Craddock, daughter and co-heir of George Craddock of Cavershall Castle, Staffordshire, Esquire, in 1658.[23] Had Sir Orlando wished to bridle his heir, the resettlement provided a perfect opportunity. However, Sir Orlando did not employ the trustees to ensure that the patrimony would descend to his unborn grandson. Part of the Bridgeman estate,[24] and the Morton inheritance, was settled upon John for life, followed by a jointure estate in Mary. A contingent remainder was limited to their male issue, but no trustees were appointed to protect the entail. In addition, Sir Orlando retained a life interest in the manor of Lady Hall in Great Lever, a moiety of the manor of Bolton and the capital messuage and demesne of Halgh and Tonge. Upon his death, a life estate was limited to John followed by an entail in his heirs male; but again no trustees were invoked to protect the contingent entail. Thus the reputed inventor of the strict settlement was chary in its use to protect his own patrimony. It was not until 1670, upon executing Articles of Agreement upon the marriage of his younger son, that Sir Orlando adopted the strict settlement.[25]

That Sir Orlando Bridgeman did not employ strict settlements early on to secure his own estate should not of course lead us to the conclusion that he did not develop the mechanics. However, this evidence does tend to suggest that he must have had some reservations about its use even in periods of political uncertainty. Since none of Bridgeman's professional papers appear to have survived, his reputation as inventor of the assurance clearly rests upon the posthumous publication of his precedents, which contain examples of strict settlements.[26] It remains to be considered how much reliance should be placed upon this slender thread of evidence.

There are salient considerations which suggest that such reliance

23 Mary Craddock was the daughter of his second wife by her first marriage: Bradford Papers, Weston Park, Class 5/7: Marriage Settlement, 23 and 24 March 1658.
24 Five messuages in Park Eyton, Denbighshire and the manor of Castle Bromwich, Warwickshire.
25 Bradford Papers, Weston Park, Class 5/7: Articles of Agreement, 28 April 1670. The actual settlement was post-nuptial. It recites the Articles and follows them in detail: *Ibid.*: Marriage Settlement, 16 September 1674.
26 Sir Orlando died in 1674; the first edition of *Bridgeman's conveyances* appeared in 1682.

is unwarranted. In the first place, Bridgeman's conveyancing book was not the first to include strict settlements. The mechanics of the strict settlement appeared in print nearly a decade before *Bridgeman's conveyances*. In 1674, George Billinghurst of Gray's Inn published a manual containing numerous clauses which might be included in family settlements.[27] One particular option was: 'A way to preserve contingent uses in case the particular Estate determine before they come in Esse'.[28] The mechanics suggested by Billinghurst were similar to those which were later to appear in *Bridgeman's conveyances*. A life estate was limited in the groom (with a jointure provision if desired) followed by an entail male. After the life estate in the groom, the author advised the inclusion of the following clause: 'And from and after the determination of the Estate of the said A. B. [the life tenant] to the use of the said C. B. and E. F. and their heirs for and during the natural life of the said A. B. to the end and purpose, and in trust to preserve the contingent remainders hereinafter mentioned.'[29] There can be no doubt that the limitation created a trust to preserve contingent remainders. I am not attempting to suggest here that the strict settlement was developed by such an obscure member of the legal profession,[30] but merely to place the publication of *Bridgeman's conveyances* in the proper historical perspective: it was not the first conveyancing book to suggest the use of trustees to preserve contingent remainders.

Secondly, nearly all late-seventeenth-century printed precedent books contain examples of strict settlements. The publication of *Bridgeman's conveyances* preceded, likewise by about a decade, the appearance of another conveyancing precedent book containing examples of strict settlements. In 1695, *The modern conveyancer* published settlements including limitations to trustees to preserve remainders.[31] Furthermore, in 1702, an index to conveyancing precedents was published.[32] Admittedly, it refers to strict settle-

---

27 *Arcania clericalia: or the mysteries of clerkship explained* (London, 1674).
28 *Ibid.*, 81 (marginal note).
29 *Ibid.*
30 Little is known about George Billinghurst. He was admitted to Gray's Inn on 29 May 1647: *The register of admissions to Gray's Inn*, ed. J. Foster (London, 1889), 245. The book attained some prominence, as it was cited nearly thirty years later as a useful manual in the Preface to *Conveyancer's assistant and director: being a treatise containing tables to all sorts of conveyances* (London, 1702).
31 *The modern conveyancer* (London, 1695), 225–40; 241–4; 416–27; 436–56.
32 *Conveyancer's assistant.*

ments in *Bridgeman's conveyances*; but it also directs conveyancers to strict settlements in three other precedent books.[33]

One must wonder whether innovations in conveyancing were actually disseminated through the various published works at all. A number of precedent books were printed in the period during which the strict settlement was developed, but none contain examples of the innovation.[34] Indeed, archaic forms were included; and it would appear that conveyancing books generally printed established rather than innovative assurances.[35] By the time *Bridgeman's conveyances* was published, the strict settlement had become the most common form of marriage settlement in Kent and Northamptonshire.[36] Aside from the clause in Billinghurst's *Arcania clericalia*, no printed conveyancing book contains examples of strict settlements during the initial period of their adoption by landed society.

A further consideration tends to suggest that it would be inappropriate to attribute the innovation to Bridgeman solely because of the publication of his conveyances. It concerns the relationship between printed conveyancing books and the practitioner during the period. Undoubtedly, printed precedent books were produced for professional consumption, but it is also clear that the practitioners kept their own manuscript notebooks containing copies of settlements, deeds and various other instruments. It is likely that they drew upon both sources to satisfy the needs of their

33 *Ibid.*, 412, referring to 205–11 in *Bridgeman's conveyances*; and 422, referring to the *Modern conveyancer, scriveners guide* (I have not been able to find a reference to this volume), and *Compleat conveyancer: a collection of presidents for conveyances* (London, 1701).

34 I have surveyed what I believe to be all of the precedent books published between 1650 and 1670: William Sheppard, *The touchstone of common assurances* (London, 1651); Thomas Fidell, *A perfect guide for the studious young lawyer* (London, 1654); *The perfect conveyancer: or several select and choice presidents* (London, 1655); William Sheppard, *The president of presidents: or one general president for common assurances by deeds* (London, 1655); John Herne, *The modern assurancer: or the clerk's directory* (London, 1658); *Exact clark and scrivener: a compendium of all manner of precedents now in use* (London, 1659); *Exact book of most approved precedents* (London, 1663); *Complete clark, containing the best forms of all sorts of precedents for conveyances and assurances* (London, 1664); Richard Hutton, *The young clarks guide, or an exact collection of choice English precedents* (London, 1670).

35 A marriage settlement in Herne, *The Modern assurancer*, 128, employs an invalid perpetuity. Dr. John Baker suggests that early-sixteenth-century printed books are 'backward-looking if not distinctly out of date'; *Spelman's reports*, II, 204.

36 See below, Chapter 5.

clients. Indeed, *Bridgeman's conveyances* is merely the publication of the manuscripts of a prominent practitioner. But other manuscript precedent books of the period survive which, like Bridgeman's collection, contain both strict settlements and other forms of conveyance.[37] The way in which practitioners employed both printed precedent books and their own manuscript notebooks can be illustrated by reference to a law commonplace book of the mid-seventeenth century.[38] The anonymous compiler of the commonplace book indexed nine printed conveyancing books within. But in addition to these printed sources, he refers to 'My manuscripts of conveyances in a large fo.'.[39] With the regard to the dissemination of the strict settlement, this particular commonplace book is of interest. None of the nine printed precedent books contained examples of strict settlements. Under the general heading 'Trusts', there is an entry entitled 'Trusts not to destroy contingent uses' and reference is made to 'my manuscript conveyances'.[40] When this practitioner sought to draft a strict settlement, he referred to his personal collection of manuscripts rather than to a printed conveyancing book.

Manuscript precedent books were probably compiled both to serve as records of instruments drafted and as a reference for future use. There is evidence to suggest that they were often passed down from one generation to the next and were updated to take into account developments in the law and in conveyancing practice. A manuscript notebook in the possession of John Poole during the reign of Charles I contains settlements drafted in the time of Elizabeth.[41] Some of the instruments include clauses of perpetuity, and Poole duly noted the judgments which rendered them invalid.[42] In addition to providing forms to employ on appropriate occasions, precedent books also served as instruction manuals. Poole's notebook, for example, contains a section outlining the appropriate words to create various estate tails.[43] Given the manner in which

37 B.L., Harleian MS 2053, fos. 13–45; Inner Temple Library, Barrington MS 27, fos. 152–4; C.U.L. Add. MS 6235, fos. 125–7.
38 Inner Temple Library, Barrington MS 80.
39 *Ibid.*, fo. 1.
40 *Ibid.*, fo. 40.
41 B.L., Add. MS 36077, styled 'Conveyancing book of John Poole, Esq., temp Charles I'.
42 *Ibid.*, fos. 13–17, 18–22.
43 *Ibid.*, fo. 57.

these notebooks were compiled and exploited by practitioners, it seems inappropriate to attribute the innovation to Bridgeman solely because this particular conveyancing book subsequently achieved prominence.

If the widespread use of trustees to preserve contingent remainders preceded the appearance of the mechanics in precedent books, an alternative means of circulation must have been responsible for its dissemination. One can only speculate, but quite possibly the centralization of both the legal profession and legal education in London provided the means. Sufficient evidence exists for an example to be constructed. William Buckby, a Bedfordshire gentleman, was admitted to the Inner Temple in November 1652. Little is known of his career except that he was made a Bencher in 1677 and a Serjeant in 1680.[44] His manuscript notebook, styled 'My Book of Legal Precedents', survives and contains numerous marriage settlements executed in the late 1640s and 1650s.[45] Clearly, the dates of the settlements render it unlikely that he was the draftsman. Rather it seems probable that he came across them while a student, and copied them for future reference. In addition to copies of settlements, the book contains a discourse upon the 'Settlement of an Estate not to be destroyed'.[46] Here Buckby noted the structure of the strict settlement, and set out the legal rationale for each particular limitation. Both this detailed account of the workings of the strict settlement and the actual copying of settlements employing trustees to preserve contingent remainders by a student of the Inner Temple suggest that knowledge of the strict settlement was rather widespread amongst aspiring young members of the legal profession in the 1650s. Perhaps men such as Buckby provided the means for disseminating innovative forms of conveyance.

Having attempted to assess the role of Sir Orlando Bridgeman in the development of the strict settlement, we may now consider the settlements of Sir Geoffrey Palmer, Blackstone's other candidate for inventor of the strict settlement. As with Bridgeman, there is a dearth of substantive evidence linking Sir Geoffrey with the inspiration of the mechanics, but a survey of his own settlements indicates that he employed trustees to preserve contingent remainders in many of his own marriage and family settlements. In

44 *Students admitted to the Inner Temple, 1547–1660* (London, 1877), 345.
45 N.R.O. M(TM) 575.
46 *Ibid.*, fos. 160–1.

1654, Palmer executed a settlement upon the marriage of his eldest son and heir, Lewis, with Jane, daughter of Robert Palmer of Carlton Scroops, a Lincolnshire squire.[47] The settlement was only a partial one. A significant segment of the patrimony, the fee farm rents of the manor of Kettering, valued at £66 7s 10d, was settled upon Lewis in the conventional life estate-entail mode. But the manor of Carlton and various other premises were settled upon Sir Geoffrey for life, followed by a jointure estate in his wife, with remainder to Lewis for life. The contingent entail following Lewis's life interest was protected by trustees to preserve contingent remainders. Moreover, should Lewis die without male issue, a life estate-entail disposition protected by trustees to preserve contingent remainders was limited to Sir Geoffrey's younger son, Edward.

Perhaps the impetus behind Palmer's employment of the strict settlement upon his eldest son's marriage was Lewis's spendthrift nature. By 1664, Lewis was in debt to the tune of £3,000, and Sir Geoffrey executed a further settlement in the form of a lease for fifteen years of recently purchased land to trust to raise money to pay the debt.[48] Portions for Lewis's daughter and his three younger sons were also directed. The next day another family settlement was executed with two dispositions, both employing trustees to preserve contingent remainders.[49] Part of the settled premises directly devolved upon Lewis's eldest son, Robert, at the death of Sir Geoffrey, while part was settled upon Lewis for life with trustees to preserve contingent remainders. To further protect the settlement, Lewis's interest was followed by a life estate in Robert as vested remainderman.

In January 1667, Palmer revoked this family settlement in favour of a more comprehensive one.[50] No estate of freehold was limited to Lewis, but a trust was created to allow him to receive the profits of one-third of the manor of Westhall in Carlton. After the death of Lewis, a twenty-year trust was established to discharge the debts and legacies of Sir Geoffrey. Upon the determination of the trust, the land was settled upon Robert Palmer for life; Robert's life estate was followed by an entail in his heirs male protected by trustees to

47 L.R.O. Palmer MSS 623, 624.
48 L.R.O. Palmer MS 625.
49 L.R.O. Palmer MS 626.
50 L.R.O. Palmer MSS 627, 630.

preserve contingent remainders. The bulk of the estate, however, was settled upon Sir Geoffrey's two daughters and their male issue. Life estates were granted to each daughter with entails secured in their eldest sons. Each disposition was protected by trustees to preserve contingent remainders. By the time of his death in 1670, Sir Geoffrey Palmer had disposed of most of his estate by *inter vivos* settlement with all of the entails settled in unborn persons secured by trustees to preserve contingent remainders.[51]

If Sir Geoffrey was a keen exponent of the innovation to assure his own estates, there is less evidence that he advised his clients to employ the strict settlement in their own marriage settlements. In 1655, Sir Geoffrey's close friend Abel Barker married his niece Mary, daughter of Alexander Noel, Esquire.[52] From extant correspondence, it is clear that Barker employed Palmer to draft the marriage settlement.[53] This was Barker's second marriage; and his first marriage had produced a male heir. Palmer's first draft was the life estate-entail model with a jointure provision, but without trustees to preserve contingent remainders.[54] The entail was secured in the male issue produced by the marriage. In the margin, Sir Geoffrey penned the following note: 'The son by the first marriage being heir at law unless some entails be limited for the issue of the second wife   None will descend to him   And this is a common entail which may be cut of[f] by Fine   Nevertheless if Mr Barker does not agree it may be omitted.'[55] In fact, Abel Barker did not agree, and a second draft was offered with a life estate, jointure estate, followed by a fee simple interest in his right heirs.[56] This was the form adopted in the settlement.[57]

Although Sir Geoffrey appears not to have advised his close

51 In his will, Sir Geoffrey recited the following: 'I have disposed my Lands of Inheritance (which by Gods Blessing upon my endeavours are much more than I derived from my ancestors) by Acts during my life time. And I doe humbly bessech God his blessing may continue and goe along with them according to the uses and interests, therof declared or limited.' P.R.O. PROB 11/333, 81.
52 L.R.O. Barker MS DE 730/1, no. 43: Marriage Certificate, 6 September 1655.
53 L.R.O. Barker MS DE 730/4, no. 228: Abel Barker to Geoffrey Palmer, 23 August 1655. In a letter Barker thanks Palmer for interceding on his behalf in his suit for Palmer's niece 'at request of all ye concerned, if ye would be pleased to draw Joynture'. On 2 September, Barker wrote to his prospective father-in-law, Alexander Noel: 'Last night my servt returned with the writings from Mr P. whom Thursday he left in good health.'
54 L.R.O. Barker MS DE 730/5, 38–44.
55 *Ibid.*, 41.
56 *Ibid.*, 46–51.
57 L.R.O. Conant MS DG 11/960.

friend, Abel Barker, to employ a strict settlement, there is evidence
that he drafted strict settlements rather early on. In 1676, the case of
Brisco v. *The Countess of Banbury*[58] came before Lord Chancellor
Nottingham. The case is a complex one, involving the rights of a
mortgagee on premises settled with a power of revocation. At issue
was a post-nuptial strict settlement executed on 29 January 1651,
and Nottingham noted: 'and I observed that Sir Geoffrey Palmer
was of counsel in all those deeds'.[59]

Thus the Banbury settlements and the dates of the settlements in
Bridgeman's conveyances demonstrate that both of these eminent
lawyers drafted strict settlements. Yet as we have seen, there is a
dearth of substantive evidence to suggest that either conveyancer
developed the strict settlement. That Sir Geoffrey employed the
strict settlement to assure his patrimony early on while Sir Orlando
was more cautious does not, of course, lead to the conclusion that it
was Palmer rather than Bridgeman who developed the device of
trustees to preserve contingent remainders. Indeed a marriage
settlement[60] found amongst the many preserved in the Northamptonshire Record Office tends to suggest that the innovation may
rightly be attributed to neither of these eminent lawyers. Moreover,
the date of the settlement, November 1641, tends to undermine the
suggestion by Lord Hardwicke that the strict settlement was
developed in response to the uncertainties of the civil war.[61]

The pre-civil war settlement in question was executed by a rather
obscure Northamptonshire squire, John Thornton of Brookole,
upon his marriage with Hester, daughter of William Priestly of
Eisenden, Herts., Esquire. In the settlement, Thornton reserved a
life estate in himself, followed by a jointure provision in his bride,
with the remainder in the heirs male produced by the marriage.
After the limitation in tail, a further clause was added: 'and for want
of such issue to the use of the said Sir John Gore and William
Priestly and their heirs during the natural life of the said John
Thornton'.[62] No further explanation of the trust appears in the
settlement.

58 *Nottingham's Chancery cases*, case no. 522.
59 *Ibid.*, 388.
60 Sequence no. 229.
61 See above, pp. 58–9. Although not himself embracing this view, the earliest
   example of a strict settlement uncovered by Professor Habakkuk was executed
   in 1647, a date which conforms to the Blackstone–Hardwicke view: Habakkuk,
   'Marriage settlements', 18, fn. 1.
62 Sequence no. 229.

Admittedly, two queries may be raised as to whether the trust was actually one to protect contingent remainders. First, it may be argued that no specific mention is made of preserving the entail in the unborn son. Yet not all strict settlements did so; an example of a strict settlement in *The modern conveyancer* reputed to be 'per Sir Geof Palmer' also omits the purpose of the trust.[63] Secondly, the trustees to preserve contingent remainders appears after the entail male rather than after the life estate. Perhaps this is sloppy draftmanship, because by the terms of the limitation the estate in the trustees exists 'during the natural life of the said John Thornton'. The placement of a limitation in a settlement was not crucial; clearly it would have prevented the life tenant from defeating the entail regardless of where it appeared in the conveyance. Thus it would seem that the concept of preserving contingent remainders by trustees preceded the civil war. Unfortunately, it is not possible to ascertain the draftsman of this particular settlement; yet it seems unlikely that it was either Bridgeman or Palmer.

To the historian of conveyancing practice, however, the inventor of the mechanics is not nearly as important as the form employed. The method used to secure the entail, the implementation of a trust, may be explained by what has been termed the 'revival of equitable estates'.[64] After the enactment of the Statute of Uses in 1536,[65] equitable estates did not disappear altogether, since active uses and uses of copyholds and leaseholds were not within the ambit of the statute. During the reign of Elizabeth, the trust began to emerge once again as a device which might be employed to temper the rigours of the common law. Trusts, for example, were employed to enable married women to hold property independently of their spouses.[66] In addition, they were implemented in marriage settlements to secure the interests of the infant *en ventre sa mere* until parliamentary intervention obviated the need for such protection.[67] Later they would be used to secure portions for younger sons and daughters.[68]

63 *The modern conveyancer* (London, 1695), 418–27, 'To the use of the said E. R. for and during the term of the Natural life of the said T. A. jun [the life tenant]'.
64 D. E. C. Yale, 'The revival of equitable estates in the seventeenth century', *Cambridge Law Journal* (1957).
65 27 Hen. VIII c. 10.
66 Cioni, thesis, 15.
67 Sequence nos. 35, 46, 61, 62, 64, 67, 72, 73, 81, 82, 86, 91, 95, 142, 212, 227, 228, 241, 242, 243, 244, 245, 247, 248, 249, 250, 251, 255, 257, 258, 259, 261, 263, 267. The statute is 10 William III c. 22.
68 See below, Chapter 6.

Thus lawyers once again began to employ equitable estates to accomplish that which the machinery of the common law would not allow. After the enactment of the Statute of Tenures in 1660,[69] the judges were less hostile towards the implementation of trusts, since their potential for avoiding feudal revenues was no longer a concern.[70] Consequently, it may not be necessary to hark back to *Cholmley's Case* to find the 'germ of the device'. Conveyancers, and perhaps even Sir Orlando Bridgeman, 'the Great Oracle . . . of the whole Nation in Matters of Law',[71] may well have developed the mechanics of the strict settlement by invoking contemporary notions of the flexibility of the trust.

Speculation as to the origins of the strict settlement aside, we may now tread upon firmer terrain, and investigate the case law which established both the quality of the estate in the trustees and their obligations under the settlement. Modern legal historians have stressed the importance of two common law cases, *Duncomb* v. *Duncomb* and *Dormer* v. *Parkhurst*, which adjudged the remainder in the trustees to be vested, and thereby secured the viability of the strict settlement.[72] That the developments in Chancery have largely been ignored is somewhat surprising, since litigation involving strict settlements was entertained in this forum prior to actions at common law. While it may be argued that the decision in *Duncomb* prompted the Chancellor to protect the interests of the contingent remainderman, the Chancery cases are of interest because the court was considering the question of the extent of the protection to be offered. But as is commonly the case in matters of law, questions of doctrine and remedy are often interrelated. By enforcing the trust, successive Chancellors were in fact defining the nature of the interest conferred upon the trustees. Thus, by the time the case of *Dormer* came before the common law judges, Chancery had already *assumed* the estate in the trustees to be vested. Perhaps this is why the judges were forced to bend the rules regarding contingent remainders to reach a similar conclusion.

But even the argument that it was the decision in *Duncomb* which prompted the Chancellor to protect the remainderman against disloyal trustees may well be suspect. There is evidence to suggest

---

69 12 Car. II c. 24.
70 Yale, 'Revival of equitable estates', 85.
71 *Bridgeman's conveyances*. Preface by Thomas Johnson.
72 See, for example, *H.E.L.*, VII, 112, and Simpson, *Land law*, 215. The report of *Duncomb* (1697) is 3 Lev. 437, and *Dormer* (1740), 6 Bro. P.C. 351.

that Chancery undertook to provide a remedy for the disappointed male heir long before the 1690s. In 1675, William Sheppard wrote:

And therefore Contingent Uses may be extinguished or suspended at this day. As where a man seised of Land in Fee . . . make a feoffment of his land to diverse Feoffes to the use of them and their Heirs during the life of A [the life tenant] and after to the use of the first Son that A shall beget, and the Heirs male of the body of such first son . . . If in these cases the Feoffe make a Feoffment over before the contingent Uses happen to be in use, as before A hath any Son albeit to one that hath notice of these uses, yet the uses are destroyed for ever, and the Feoffies cannot enter and revive them contrary to their own Feoffment. And if in these cases, the Feoffe, before the contingent remainder vest, be dissessed, hereby the Uses will be suspended; but thereby the re-entry of the Feoffies, the ancient Uses will be revived again. And therefore if the Feoffies [in this case] release to the Dissessor, and so bar themselves of their entry, the uses will be gone forever, and cannot be revived. And the party grieved will have no remedy [in these cases] but in Chancery against the Feoffies for breach of their trusts.[73]

According to Sheppard, then, it would appear that rather early on the Chancellor protected the trust to preserve contingent remainders in the same manner as any other trust. Equity provided a remedy for nonfeasance or complicity on the part of the trustees to preserve contingent remainders; and it did so long before the quality of estate in the trustees was established at common law. Bearing this in mind, let us now consider the development in legal doctrine, turning first to the common law cases and then to the parallel developments in Chancery.

The first case to consider is *Duncomb* v. *Duncomb*, in which a widow brought a writ of dower claiming her thirds in land settled 'to husband for life, remainder to J. S. for the life of the husband, remainder to the heirs male of the husband, remainder to G. D. in tail'; husband died without issue and G. D. entered. In maintaining that the estate should be subject to dower, counsel for the widow, argued that the remainder to J. S. was 'no more than a possibility; so that if her husband committed a forfeiture, J. S. might take advantage thereof for preservation of remainders'.[74] Citing *Lewis Bowles's Case*[75] counsel further contended that the whole estate tail was vested in the husband until the birth of male issue when it

73 Sheppard, *Grand abridgement*, vol. III, part IV, p. 186.
74 (1697), 3 Lev. 437.
75 (1616), 11 Co. Rep. 79b.

would 'divide' into two distinct estates; the widow was therefore entitled to claim dower out of the lands under settlement. But the court rejected this argument, and 'hastily gave judgment for the tenant'.[76]

No lengthy exposition of the legal rationale which supported the judgment was offered by the court, and its absence is conspicuous. Perhaps there were doubts as to the consistency of the judgment with accepted legal doctrine regarding contingent remainders. Indeed, in a subsequent case Lord Hardwicke considered the result to be appropriate, 'though Mr Justice Levinz [the reporter] seemed even to doubt it there'.[77]

Eighteenth-century commentators attempted to rationalize the decision in *Duncomb* either by altering the notion of what rendered a remainder contingent, or by circumventing the issue entirely. Fearne appeared to ignore his own definition of the 'first sort' of contingent remainder, those which commence upon a contingent determination of the precedent estate, and agreed that the remainder was vested.[78] No longer was the emphasis to be upon whether the enjoyment of the estate commenced upon the occurrence of a contingency; Fearne concluded that so long as the precedent estate must determine some time in the future upon an event which must occur and was limited to a person *in esse*, the remainder was considered vested.[79] That the remainderman *would not* come into enjoyment of his interest if the precedent estate determined upon that event certain to occur seemed no longer relevant. In contrast, Charles Viner conceded that the estate commenced upon a possibility; yet he circumvented the issue by offering a different rationale for the decision. Viner contended that the interest in the trustees 'was such an interposing estate between first estate limited to A for life and the last estate limited to him in tail that A could be considered as no more than a bare tenant for life'.[80] Extremely neat legal reasoning; yet one finds no support for his explanation in the report of the opinion, nor is it consistent with the reasoning in *Lewis Bowles's Case*.

The next occasion for the common law judges to consider the

76 (1697), 3 Lev. 437.
77 *Hooker* v. *Hooker* (1735), Cas. T. Hard. 13, 17.
78 Fearne, *On contingent remainders*, 5. See quote above, pp. 56–7.
79 Fearne, *On contingent remainders*, 218–20.
80 Viner, *Abridgement*, XVIII, 415–16.

nature of the remainder conferred upon the trustees to preserve contingent remainders came in the case of *Dormer* v. *Parkhurst*.[81] Upon a writ of error, the case was argued in the House of Lords in 1740. Because the nature of the interest of the tenant in possession was so crucial to the outcome, it is essential to set out the facts in some detail. The settlement executed in 1662 in substance ran as follows: '[after several precedent estates] to the use of A for 99 years, if he should so long live, and from and after the sooner determination of this estate, to trustees during the life of A to preserve contingent remainders, and after the end or other sooner determination of the estate, remainder to the heirs male of A in succession, remainder to B in tail'. A came into possession and together with his eldest son levied a fine to create a tenant to the *preacipe*, and then suffered a recovery; thereafter both A and his son died without issue, and the next remainderman (B) entered. At issue was whether the 'freehold' was in the life tenant and the remainderman or in the trustees. This point was crucial, for if the trustees had seisin of a vested interest, then A and his son could not create a tenant to the *preacipe* without them; the recovery, therefore, would not bar subsequent remaindermen.

Thus the case turned upon the nature of the estate in the trustees, and this point was governed in part by the quality of interest granted to A. But first each side put forward its interpretation of the interest settled upon the trustees. The gravamen of the appellant's argument was that the estate in the trustees must be considered contingent, since it could only be vested if it came into effect upon every determination of the precedent estate. Under the settlement, it was averred, the estate in the trustees took effect only upon the 'sooner determination' of the term of 99 years determinable upon the death of A.[82] Such an argument was not unreasonable, given the conventional definition of a contingent remainder, but it ignored the modification of doctrine implicit in the decision in *Duncomb*. Counsel for the defendant in error learned the lesson of *Duncomb*, and argued that the trustees were *in esse* and that the precedent estate must end either by the death of A, 'effluxion of time' or by a

81 (1740), 6 Bro. P.C. 351. The opinion of Chief Justice Willes is set out more fully in (1741), 3 Atk. 135, and (1741), Willes 327. Procedural matters regarding whether retrials of actions in ejectment may be granted are reported in (1738), 3 Andr. 315, and (1738), 2 Stra. 1105.
82 6 Bro. P.C. 351, 353.

forfeiture. To render the remainder contingent because of the words
'sooner determination' was absurd; this was implied in every term
of years, because such estates were subject to surrender or
forfeiture.[83]
   In his opinion Chief Justice Willes agreed with counsel for the
defendant in error. Considering the remainder in the trustees to be
vested, he applied similar reasoning: the trustees were *in esse* and
capable of taking upon the determination of the precedent estate,
and the remainder did not commence upon any collateral event. But
the manner in which he described how the vested estate passed to
the trustees was quite novel, and it depended upon the interest in A.
Chief Justice Willes presented a case:

A, tenant in fee grants an estate to B for 99 years determinable on his life;
Supposing B outlive the term, or surrender, or forfeit, no one I believe will
say but that A may not enjoy the estate again. If so then a contingent
freehold was in him during the life of B for it could not be in B, because he
had only a chattel interest and it could not be in anyone else. And if it were
in A it must be a vested interest, for it was never out of him, . . . no one can
say but that he might grant it over, and if he do it must be of the same nature
it was when it was in A, and consequently a vested freehold. And this case I
have but is expressly held to be law . . . in *Cholm(l)ey's Case* . . .[84]

Thus the estate in the trustees was vested, because it emanated from
the reversion which the grantor retained in the conveyance of a
term. According to Chief Justice Willes, this nicety required that
the trustees join to bar the remainder:

To say . . . that it was the intent of the parties that the first tenant for 99
years and the first remainderman in tail should have it in their power to bar
all the remainders . . . is without any foundation. If this had been the intent
of the parties, A would have been made a tenant for life; for in that case it
would not have been in his power without the trustees to have barred his
first son, but he and his son when of age might have barred all remainders.[85]

Consequently, the opinion created a distinction between the types of
precedent estate settled; yet, as Viner remarked, the same reasoning
could apply when the grantor settled a life estate, since 'the limitor
has notwithstanding an interest remaining in him to enter upon

83 *Ibid.*, 354–5.
84 Willes 327, 339.
85 *Ibid.*, 333.

alienation, forfeiture, etc. which interest when conveyed to the trustees is a remainder or legal estate'.[86]

Thus it was this example enunciated by Lord Coke in *Cholmley's Case*, and not the one cited by Lord Hardwicke, which ultimately served as the rationale for the remainder in the trustees to be considered vested by the common law courts. Moreover, policy reasons supported this construction. The most crucial concern dealt with estate resettlement. To construe the freehold to be in the trustees would be, according to the appellants, 'very inconvenient', since it would preclude resettlement by the father and his eldest son without the consent of the trustees.[87] But as we have seen, Chief Justice Willes considered this inconvenience to conform with the interest of the settlor; and since his goal did not conflict with the developing rules against perpetuities, the court must honour his wishes.[88]

Having established the way in which the common law courts came to regard the estate in the trustees as vested, we may now consider the manner in which Chancery undertook to protect the interest of the contingent remainderman. To some extent these developments were interrelated. Even though it would appear that Chancery protected the trust long before *Duncomb*, the determination by the Court of Common Pleas in *Duncomb* to consider the estate in the trustees vested was tantamount to accepting in principle that a landowner could control the destiny of the patrimony until his grandson reached the age of majority. Yet, to implement the principle, it was necessary for the Chancellor to exercise his jurisdiction over trusts to compel the trustee to perform his duties under the settlement by providing a remedy for nonfeasance.

The Chancellor was quite willing to protect the interest of the contingent remainderman, and during the forty years after *Dun-*

---

86 Viner, *Abridgement*, XVIII, 416. Amongst the sixty-five Kentish strict settlements executed by the groom or his family only twelve employ the 'term of 99 years' disposition found in the settlement in *Dormer*. Of these, thirty-seven (58.3%) were executed by the groom. Since the groom employed this form as often as did fathers in resettlements, it would not appear that settlors consciously attempted to use this form to preclude the tenant in possession and the remainderman from joining to break the settlement.

87 6 Bro. P.C. 351, 354.

88 Willes 327, 333. Counsel on the other side argued that to consider the limitation to the trustees to be a contingent remainder would 'endanger most of the family settlements in the kingdom'. 6 Bro. P.C. 351, 355. Willes was aware of the unsettling effect of holding the remainder to be contingent: Willes 327, 339.

comb, the bounds of protection were established. In the end, the Chancellor determined that the trust protected only the first contingent remainderman, the issue produced by the marriage, and not the ultimate remaindermen, by allowing the tenant in possession to join with his eldest son to break the existing settlement. But he required the trustees to join in the conveyance, and in so doing the Chancellor defined the nature of the estate in the trustees long before *Dormer*. Thus it might be argued that by 1740 decisions in Chancery had presented the common law judges with a *fait accompli* regarding the quality of the estate in the trustees.

When Chancery protection commenced is less certain. Although Sheppard maintained that Chancery was protecting the trust before 1675, others offered different opinions. For example, in his argument in the *Duke of Norfolk's Case* Sir Henry Pollexfen contended that 'Contingent Estates were never . . . yet favoured in Equity: Trustees for preserving Contingent Remainders are not punished in Equity though they break their Trusts and destroy them.'[89] Certainly complicity on the part of trustees to break the settlement before the birth of male issue was not unknown. In February 1665, the Earl of Cork, trustee to preserve contingent remainders in a settlement executed upon the marriage of his daughter Elizabeth with the third Earl of Thanet, joined with his son-in-law in a deed of revocation which extinguished the contingent estate limited to the heirs male produced by the marriage.[90]

Yet, the tenor of Chancery opinions before *Duncomb* tends to support Sheppard's view. For example, even before the common law courts determined that the estate in the trustees was vested, the Chancellor expressed some doubt as to whether it was appropriate to compel a trustee to join in a sale of settled estates to pay debts even where there was little probability of issue. In *Davies* v. *Weld*, Lord Keeper North was faced with this dilemma, and refused to render such a decree 'for he had known, where people had been married near twenty years without issue and after had children'.[91] Precedents,[92] however, were cited, but the Lord Keeper was unmoved, although he allowed counsel leave to supply him with

89 (1681), Pollex, 223, 250.
90 K.A.O. U 455 T282.
91 (1683), 1 Vern. 182.
92 *Digby* v. *Cornwallis* (1671), 3 Ch. Rep. 72; and *Sir John Tufton's Case* (unreported). In neither case is it clear that strict settlements were involved. Lord Nottingham noted that the settlement employed trustees to preserve contingent remainders, *Prolegomena*, 266.

further authority. However, in *Platt* v. *Spugg*, the Master of the Rolls, at the behest of a plaintiff who entered into a contract to purchase land under strict settlement, ordered the trustees to join in the sale of the estate.[93] No reason was stated for the decree, but plaintiff's argument was indeed persuasive: as the land was encumbered the settlement had only been of an equity of redemption (i.e. the premises had been mortgaged before the settlement was executed); since the settlor was unable to meet the obligation, the mortgagee was prepared to foreclose, and foreclosure would bind the settlor's issue. Thus there was little point in refusing to allow the trustees to join in the conveyance.

With the decision in *Duncomb*, however, the attitude of Chancery regarding the duty of the trustees altered. But the alteration may have been due to a change in the nature of the cases brought before the Chancellor rather than to the determination in the Common Pleas. Previously, the court had been faced with petitioners requesting to break the settlement; thereafter cases arose where the contingent remainderman, deprived of his interest, petitioned the court for relief. It now became necessary to formulate a policy; and in *Pye* v. *Gorge*, Lord Keeper Harcourt declared such complicity to be a 'plain breach of trust'.[94] But the Lord Keeper went even further to suggest an appropriate remedy; in cases where the grantee entered into conveyance, either voluntarily or with notice, Lord Harcourt determined that the purchaser took subject to the trust: 'And tho' it was objected, that this had been only *obiter* said in equity, and that there never was any precedent of a decree in such a case: Lord Keeper said it was so very plain and reasonable, that if there was no precedent in this case he would make one.'[95] Since a son had been born before the trustees entered into the particular conveyance before the court, the Lord Keeper's determination was *dicta*; yet the case was an important one in establishing the policy of equity towards disloyal trustees. Trustees who entered into conveyances to defeat the interest of the contingent remainderman were hereafter to be considered in breach of trust; and purchasers with notice took subject to the trust.

What was left to be determined was the breadth of the protective

93 (1693), 2 Vern. 303.
94 (1710), 1 P. Wms. 128. Affirmed by the House of Lords (1712), 7 Bro. P.C. 221.
   The settlement was effected by devise.
95 *Ibid.*

'umbrella' established by Chancery. In *Tipping* v. *Piggot*,[96] the Chancellor was petitioned by the heir at law of a settlor, the ultimate remainderman under a marriage settlement, to set aside a conveyance by the tenant in possession in which the trustees had joined to deprive him of his interest. Lord Chancellor Harcourt refused to grant relief and held that such conveyances should be set aside only at the behest of the first and other sons who took under the settlement as purchasers. Ultimate remaindermen were not to be protected. Later the court required the consent of a younger son before compelling the trustees to join with the tenant in possession and his eldest son to break the settlement.[97]

Lord Chancellor Cowper continued to follow this policy. In *Elie* v. *Osborne*, he declared that the trustees 'are trustees purely for the tenant in tail'.[98] Furthermore, it was Lord Cowper who first recognized that if the trustee must join in a conveyance to break a strict settlement, such as the one which was to become before the King's Bench thirty years later in *Dormer*, then their interest must be vested: '. . . for although the father was living he was but barely tenant for 99 years, if he lived so long and the estate tail vested in the eldest son in equity, but the legal estate in the trustees and their heirs.'[99] Thus, in determining the breadth of the protection provided by the trust, it was incumbent upon the Chancellor to define the nature of the separate interests conveyed by the settlement.

Although the course had been charted, there were to be some aberrations. In *Basset* v. *Clapham*, the court decreed that trustees should join to defeat a post-nuptial strict settlement.[100] In this instance, the settlor had already executed a conveyance of his estate to pay debts, and the bill had been brought by his creditors. Sir Joseph Jekyll, the Master of the Rolls, appeared reluctant to order the trustees to convey their interest, thereby destroying the contingent remainder 'this being the reverse of the purpose for

96 (1713), 1 Eq. Cas. Abr. 385.
97 *Townsend* v. *Lawson* (1726), 2 P. Wms. 380.
98 (1717), 2 Vern. 754.
99 *Ibid.*, cf. *Winnington* v. *Folley* (1718), 1 P. Wms. 536. Lord Keeper Harcourt was the first to recognize that the tenant in possession and the eldest son as remainderman in tail could break the settlement if the interests of the other parties who were provided for under the settlement were protected: *Frewin* v. *Charleton* (1712), 1 Eq. Cas. Abr. 386.
100 (1717), 1 P. Wms. 358.

which they were at first instituted'.[101] But it was argued that the settlement had been voluntary; and perhaps recognizing the potential for such settlements to defraud creditors, he decreed that the trustees should join in the conveyance to destroy the contingent remainders.

Some reconciliation of the law was in order, since counsel had been arguing that a distinction should be drawn between voluntary settlements and those based upon valuable consideration. In practice, the former were often established by devise, and the latter by marriage settlement. In *Mansell* v. *Mansell*, however, Lord Chancellor King, sitting with Chief Justice Raymond of King's Bench and Chief Baron Reynolds of the Exchequer, abolished any distinction between the two types of settlement.[102] In this case, the settlement had been created by devise 'to sister for life, remainder to trustees to preserve contingent remainders, remainder to her heirs male in tail, remainder to E. M.'; sister married Sir Edward Mansell, and both husband and wife joined with him in a conveyance to trustees to use of Sir Edward in fee; later the trustees conveyed their interest by lease and release to Sir Edward. Afterwards a son was born, and Sir Edward devised the estate 'to eldest son for life, remainder to trustees to preserve contingent remainders, remainder to the heirs male of the eldest son'. The eldest son brought in a bill in Chancery to have the settlement under the first will restored so that he would be seised of the estate as a tenant in tail rather than as a life tenant.

Three points were argued and resolved in *Mansell*. First, the feoffment by Sir Edward and his wife did not destroy the contingent remainder; and secondly, 'When the trustees joined in the lease and release to Sir Edward and his heirs, this *destroyed* the contingent remainders'.[103] Finally, the action by the trustees was a plain breach of trust.

While Lord Raymond denied Lord Cowper's determination that the eldest son in *Elie* had a vested estate in equity by contending 'that the eldest son could have no more of estate vested in him in equity than he could have in law',[104] all three accepted Cowper's determination of the nature of the estate in the father, and in the

101 *Ibid.*
102 (1732), 2 P. Wms. 678.
103 *Ibid.*, 683.
104 *Ibid.*

trustees. Although later equity would sanction the compliance of trustees in breaking settlements to further the purposes of the original settlement, the Chancellor never retreated from his characterization of the interest settled upon the trustees.[105]

Thus, by 1740, the nature of the interest in the trustees had been settled, at least in the minds of the successive Lord Chancellors. To conform with Chancery practice, it was necessary for the common law judges in *Dormer* to reshape the definition of contingent remainders;[106] to do so was no longer anathema, since protection against perpetuities had been established. Moreover, the judges were aware of the consequences of invalidating a method of settlement which was employed by a large segment of the landed class. And the strict settlement was a useful form of conveyance, providing secure financial provisions for family members, as well as stability for the patrimony over a period of time which was deemed to be reasonable.

Professor Habakkuk has contended that the strict settlement did not become the 'stock recommendation' of the conveyancer until the 'turn of the century'.[107] This assertion conforms neatly with the establishment of the nature of the estate in the trustees in *Duncomb*. However, as we have seen, Chancery intervention to protect the interest of the contingent remaindermen occurred earlier. Moreover, to hark back to the words of Bacon on perpetuities, questionable forms of conveyance were often employed merely to discourage purchasers.[108] After speculating upon the origins of the strict settlement and considering the manner in which it was accepted by the courts, the focus may now turn to the adoption of the strict settlement from its inception to 1740.

---

105 *Symance* v. *Tattam* (1737), 1 Atk. 613; and *Barnard* v. *Large* (1781), Amb. 774.
106 Clearly, the common lawyers were aware of the developments in equity. In *Mansell*, Lord Chief Justice Raymond sat with the Chancellor. Indeed, Lord Willes cites *Elie* v. *Osborne* in his opinion in *Dormer* (1741): Willes 327, 333.
107 H. J. Habakkuk, 'The English land market in the eighteenth century', in *Britain and the Netherlands*, ed. J. S. Bromley and E. H. Krossman (London, 1960), 164.
108 *Works*, VII, 623.

5

THE ADOPTION OF THE STRICT SETTLEMENT 1660–1740: KENT AND NORTHAMPTONSHIRE

One of the more difficult problems confronting legal historians interested in conveyancing practice is determining the speed and the means by which innovations in mechanics were adopted. With regard to means, it has been suggested that printed precedent books furnished the practitioner with established rather than innovative forms, and that it is therefore unlikely that they were the vehicle for transmitting novel conveyancing forms. The centralized nature of legal education and practice in early modern England, however, may have exposed lawyers to advances in mechanics such as the strict settlement. Moreover, the existence of William Buckby's manuscript notebook suggests that some practitioners became familiar with the mechanics through their London-based education.[1] Yet it must be conceded that the draftsmen of most of the settlements which will be under observation in this chapter are unknown, and it would be extreme to suggest that all were formally educated in London. While professional contacts may in the end prove to be the means by which innovation spread, a definitive answer awaits a more exhaustive study of the legal profession during the period.

With regard to the other question, how quickly innovation was disseminated, an enquiry into the use of the strict settlement in the latter half of the seventeenth century may be enlightening. Legal historians are fortunate because evidence exists which allows us to chart its adoption. Marriage settlements executed during the period survive in sufficient numbers to enable us to assess precisely how rapidly landed society embraced the innovation. By analysing the data with reference to the economic status of the settlor, the extent to which knowledge of the mechanics of the strict settlement spread

1 N.R.O. M(TM) 575, fos. 160–1; see above, p. 66.

may be determined. It is likely that the lesser landowner employed a local lawyer rather than a Londoner to handle his conveyancing; if examples of settlements with trustees to preserve contingent remainders appear early on amongst this segment of landed society, then we must conclude that information regarding the mechanics pervaded rather a broad segment of the legal profession.

Moreover, the social distribution of landowners employing strict settlements is also of interest to economic historians, because the advent of the strict settlement is considered a crucial factor in establishing the more stable pattern of landownership which they claim characterized post-Restoration England.[2] It is appropriate briefly to summarize the prevailing view, because our results may well render some of its conclusions questionable. In particular, it has been argued that the strict settlement promoted the drift of landed property towards the greater landowners by assisting in the acquisition and preservation of estates. During the period 1680 to 1740, the era of the 'rise of great estates', the acquisition of land through marriage and inheritance long considered instrumental in the rise of certain landed families came to operate according to a fixed pattern, partly as a result of the implementation of strict settlements. Although other factors such as office and the land tax also contributed to the trend, it was the strict settlement which preserved the acquisition of landowners whose economic fortunes were rising. By employing the strict settlement earlier than their lesser neighbours and by placing a larger proportion of their estate under settlement, the greater landowners 'increased the stability of the large estate relative to the small':[3] the end result was the concentration of land in fewer hands.

Thus the dissemination of the strict settlement is of interest to both legal and economic historians. Professor Habakkuk has argued that the strict settlement did not become the 'stock recommend-

---

2 The prevailing view remains the one established by Sir John Habakkuk, in 'English landownership 1680–1740', *Econ. Hist Rev.*, X (1940). It has, however, come under some criticism: C. Clay, 'Marriage, inheritance and the rise of large estates in England, 1660–1815', *Econ. Hist. Rev.*, 2nd ser. XXI (1968); B. A. Holderness, 'The English land market in the eighteenth century: the case of Lincolnshire', *Econ. Hist Rev.*, 2nd ser. XXXVII (1974); J. V. Beckett, 'English landownership in the later seventeenth and eighteenth century: the debate and the problems', *Econ. Hist. Rev.*, 2nd ser. XXX (1977).
3 Habakkuk, 'English landownership', 7.

ation of the conveyancer' until the beginning of the eighteenth century.[4] This view would appear to be supported by two relevant points. First, the mechanics of the strict settlement were not sanctioned by a court of common law until 1697.[5] Given the common lawyers' abhorrence of innovation, cautious settlors might have been reluctant to experiment with a conveyance of dubious validity. But to state what is obvious, the workings of the common law system require experimentation to precede judicial sanction; some landowners had to be sufficiently courageous to employ the innovation in order to provide a 'test case'. Our concern will be to establish their relative numbers. Secondly, some settlors may have felt that the strict settlement unduly circumscribed the powers of the life tenant to deal with his estate. It may be useful briefly to consider their misgivings.

Contemporary reservations regarding the use of the strict settlement may best be summarized by reference to a letter from Heneage Lord Finch to the Earl of Orrery.[6] From the contents of the letter it would appear that Orrery was discussing financial arrangements with the Countess of Warwick regarding a proposed match between her daughter, Anne, and Lord Finch's heir, Daniel. Apparently, the Countess favoured the execution of a strict settlement of the Finch patrimony. Although he acknowledged the reasonableness of such a demand, Lord Finch was adamant in his refusal. The objections put forward offer insight into the reservations of contemporaries regarding the strict settlement.

Lord Finch cited three. The first concerned the restriction which the strict settlement imposed upon the tenant in possession from providing a more generous endowment for his wife and their offspring than the one specified in the marriage settlement should the husband predecease his wife. Lord Finch wrote, 'As concerns my Lady Essex, if my son die before her, he could not add a shilling to her jointure or to his daughter's portions, whereas in the way I propose he could give what increase he pleaseth.'[7] Yet to the bride's family, this rigidity conferred some advantages; without a secure disposition the surviving children might find themselves in a rather

4 Habakkuk, 'The English land market'.
5 *Duncomb v. Duncomb* (1697), 3 Lev. 437. For a discussion of litigation concerning the validity of the strict settlement, see above, pp. 71–81.
6 H.M.C., *Report on the manuscripts of the late Allan George Finch* (London, 1922), II, 17–18.
7 *Ibid.*, 18.

tenuous position if their father outlived their mother and remarried. Even the heir male might be disinherited in favour of the eldest son produced by the second match. In the peerage, however, Lord Finch contended that such a 'scruple' was unfounded: 'Tis true he may live to marry again, but tis true the barony must descend upon his sons by the first wife, and that alone carries with it the necessity of leaving an estate to it . . .'[8]

There was, however, another contention, for it was believed that a strict settlement was far too inflexible a device to assure the patrimony given the uncertain economic and political climate which followed the Restoration. In particular, family circumstances might necessitate land sales. But as Lord Finch conceded, this flaw might be remedied by the inclusion of a power of revocation which would allow the tenant in possession to 'remain master of his estate'.[9] To some extent this course would be somewhat anomalous, since it would in effect nullify even the limited restraint upon alienation which a strict settlement conferred.

Finally, the contention perhaps uppermost in his mind, Lord Finch argued:

It is against nature to make the father subject to his child . . . It is against experience, and a bitter one in my family; for I have known the son of such a settlement cast away himself in marriage and then offer to disinherit his father by treating to sell the inheritance for a song while his father lived.[10]

Consequently, according to Lord Finch, employing a strict settlement considerably diminished parental authority. Indeed, the situation was reversed with the father financially at the mercy of his son.

Yet, in the end, the landed classes overcame their objections to the strict settlement, and our task is to determine when. We may do so by analysing the form employed in those settlements which comprise the data set. For establishing the frequency with which the strict settlement appears, the period under consideration (1660–1740) has been divided into equal segments. Since we are to test Professor Habakkuk's assertion that it was not until the 'turn of the century' that the employment of the strict settlement became widespread, using twenty-year periods conveniently provides a break at 1700.

8 *Ibid.*
9 *Ibid.*
10 *Ibid.*

Table 2 *Frequency distribution of the
employment of the strict settlement* (N = 142)[11]

| | Settlement form | | | |
| | Strict settlement | | Other forms | |
Time span	N	%	N	%
1660–80	26	63.4	15	36.6
1681–1700	29	78.4	8	21.6
1701–20	25	80.6	6	19.4
1721–40	25	75.8	8	24.2
Totals	105	73.9	37	26.1

Table 2 is a frequency distribution of the dissemination of the strict settlement into Kent and Northamptonshire. During the first period, limitations in trustees to preserve contingent remainders appeared in slightly less than two-thirds of the marriage settlements in the data set. However, in the second period, and therefore before the turn of the eighteenth century, the ratio rises to nearly four out of every five (78.4%). Thereafter, during the first forty years of the eighteenth century, the percentage fluctuates slightly, but not significant statistically given the size of the data set. Consequently, it was the last twenty years of the seventeenth century rather than the early eighteenth century which witnessed the transformation in the settlement habits of landowners.

The speed with which the strict settlement was adopted is striking. It was employed by a considerable majority of settlors in the first generation after it was 'invented', before the mechanics appeared in printed conveyancing books. It is therefore clear that familiarity with the mechanics was gained through other means. During the final two decades of the seventeenth century, it achieved the same relative pre-eminence that it was to enjoy during the eighteenth century. Settlors were therefore willing to experiment with a conveyance which had not yet received judicial sanction. Indeed, contemporary juristic opinion would appear to confirm the conclusion derived from our settlements. As early as 1672, Peyton Ventris (later Justice of the Court of Common Pleas) reported:

It hath been the most common way of conveyancing to prevent the disappointing of contingent Estates to make Feoffment etc., to the use of

11 Sequence nos. 46–146; 240–80.

the Husband etc., for Life, remainder to the use of Feoffees for the Life of the Husband, and so on to contingent Remainders . . . he which hath the first Estate cannot destroy the Remainder.[12]

Having determined that the strict settlement was rapidly adopted by landed families in Kent and Northamptonshire, we may now consider the distribution of its employment by the three segments of landed society defined by Professor Habakkuk.[13] By so doing, the breadth of the familiarity of the mechanics amongst country practitioners may be assessed and the nexus between the strict settlement and the proferred trend in landownership may be considered. If the segment building and consolidating their estate, the 'great magnates', tended to use the strict settlement more actively than their lesser neighbours, then its employment may well explain in part the 'rise of great estates'. If, however, the reverse is the case, or if all segments of landed society employed the strict settlement with equal frequency, then the strict settlement may well be a neutral factor in explaining the apparent trend in landownership.

Table 3 illustrates the employment of the strict settlement by Professor Habakkuk's three segments of landed society: the 'great magnates' reckoned to have estates with a rental value in excess of £2,000 per annum; the 'substantial squirearchy' with estates returning £800 to £2,000; and the 'lesser gentry' with rent rolls of under £800 per annum.[14] The settlements which comprise the data set tend to confirm Professor Habakkuk's assertion that the 'great magnates' uniformly adopted the strict settlement immediately after its invention. Yet the data also indicate that a rather large segment of the 'substantial squirearchy', that segment of landed society which was supposedly 'stable', also adopted the strict settlement rapidly; and in the period of the 'rise of great estates', nearly nine out of ten 'substantial squires' (88.9%) employed strict

12 *Lloyd* v. *Brooking* (1672), 1 Vent. 188, 189. Cf. *Hales* v. *Risley* (1674), Pollex. 369, 383.
13 Habakkuk, 'English landownership', 3.
14 *Ibid.* In placing my settlors in Habakkuk's social classifications I considered all baronets and knights as 'substantial squires', and gentlemen as 'lesser gentry'. I believe such a course justified because in those cases where rental value is set out in the settlement, I found that the social degree conformed to Habakkuk's income brackets. However, this was only a presumption. Where the amount of land settled appeared to be greater or lesser than the income bracket, I made the appropriate change in social classification.

Table 3 *Frequency of distribution of the employment of the strict settlement by social classification 1660–1740*

| | Time spans | | | | | | | | | |
| | 1660–80 | | 1681–1700 | | 1701–20 | | 1721–40 | | Totals | |
Social classification	Strict settlement %	Other forms %	Strict settlement %	Other forms %	Strict settlement %	Other forms %	Strict settlement %	Other forms %	Strict settlement %	Other forms %
'Great magnates'	100	—	100	—	100	—	100	—	100	—
'Substantial squires'	70	30	88.9	11.1	80	20	100	—	82.1	17.9
'Lesser gentry'	50	50	69.6	30.4	76.5	23.5	63.6	36.4	64.6	35.4

settlements. Consequently, it is difficult to attribute the differing economic fortunes of these two segments of landed society to the employment of this device. But what about the lower strata of landed society? According to Professor Habakkuk, it was the 'lesser gentry' who fared worst during the period 1680 to 1740; and it was at their expense that the hegemony of the 'great magnates' was fashioned.[15] Table 3 illustrates that the 'lesser gentry' adopted the strict settlement less quickly, and employed it far less frequently after 1680 than the other two segments of landed society.

Yet a closer look at the settlements of the 'lesser gentry' is revealing. If these settlements are sorted by quantity of land conveyed, two distinct patterns emerge. Many of the 'lesser gentry', particularly in Kent, continued the practice, somewhat common in the sixteenth century, of settling upon marriage only that portion of the estate which was to comprise the bride's jointure. Thus in a number of settlements of the 'lesser gentry' we often find the conveyance of a messuage, usually the capital messuage, and a few acres, an amount clearly insufficient to support a gentleman, but one which would provide a competent jointure. For the most part these settlements are not 'strict', that is to say, the entail in remainder to the eldest son is not preceded by trustees to preserve contingent remainders. If we eliminate these partial settlements

Table 4 *Frequency distribution of the employment of the strict settlement by the 'lesser gentry' settling at least a manor* (N = 52)[16]

	Settlement form			
	Strict settlement		Other forms	
Time span	N	%	N	%
1660–80	10	71.4	4	28.6
1681–1700	12	92.3	1	7.7
1701–20	10	83.3	2	16.7
1721–40	13	100	0	—
Totals	45	86.5	7	13.5

15 Habakkuk, 'English landownership', 3.
16 Sequence nos. 48, 51, 57, 58, 63, 65, 67, 69, 71, 72, 76, 82, 87, 88, 89, 94, 95, 98, 104, 107, 109, 115, 119, 122, 127, 129, 130, 132, 133, 136, 139, 140, 142, 144, 146, 240, 244, 249, 252, 253, 254, 255, 258, 260, 261, 264, 265, 266, 267, 271, 272, 273.

and include only those conveying at least a manor and appurtenances, a far different picture emerges.

A comparison between the percentages in Table 4 and those in
Table 3 indicates that a large proportion of those 'lesser gentry'
settling at least a manor and appurtenances employed the strict
settlement. Moreover, during the period of the 'rise of great
estates', 92.1% (35 out of 38) settled their patrimonies in this
manner. Indeed, this segment of the 'lesser gentry' adopted the
strict settlement as quickly as the 'substantial squires', and
employed it as frequently. The differential in employment of the
strict settlement in these three groups is so minimal that it is
unlikely that it was a significant factor in their allegedly differing
economic fortunes.

Now isolating this segment of the 'lesser gentry' requires some
defence. Admittedly, Professor Habakkuk has never argued that the
'lesser gentry' disappeared altogether; but he does create a distinction between surviving but stagnating 'substantial squires', and
disappearing 'lesser gentry'. Furthermore he has contended that
the success of the 'great magnates' may be attributed in part to their
settlement habits: they adopted the strict settlement sooner and
entailed more of their estate.[17] However, the settlements which
comprise our data set do not appear to confirm this. For example, in
two peerage settlements, the settlor retained an interest in fee in a
portion of the patrimony.[18] More significantly, however, a large
segment of the 'lesser gentry' settled their estate in the same
manner as the 'great magnates' during the period 1680 to 1740, and
employed strict settlement as often as their counterparts in the
'substantial squirearchy'. Other things being equal, if the strict
settlement was a primary factor in establishing the primacy of the
'great magnates' and the survival of the 'substantial squirearchy',
one should expect it to have also assisted those members of the
'lesser gentry' who employed it. Consequently, the period 1680 to
1740 should also have witnessed the emergence of a reasonably
healthy, though perhaps slightly diminished, 'lesser gentry'.

Our analysis of settlement practice in Kent and Northamptonshire does tend to highlight one further factor which the historian of
conveyancing must consider: regional variation. Although the strict
settlement was adopted by a broad segment of landed society in

17 Habakkuk, 'English landownership', 3–8.
18 Lord Teynham, sequence no. 105, and Viscount Falkland, sequence no. 114.

both counties, the data do suggest some differences amongst the 'lesser gentry'.[19] The distribution is tabulated in Table 5, and indicates that the Northamptonshire 'lesser gentry' adopted the strict settlement more rapidly than their Kentish counterparts. However, it must be remembered that the sample of settlements in Northamptonshire is rather small (17), and while the disparity in adoption highlighted in Table 5 is statistically significant, it is not striking except in the first time interval.

Table 5 *Frequency distribution of the employment of the strict settlement by counties: the 'lesser gentry'* (N = 53)[20]

	County			
	Kent		Northamptonshire	
Time span	N	%	N	%
1660–80	6	40	4	80
1681–1700	11	64.7	5	83.3
1701–20	8	72.7	5	83.3
1721–40	11	61.1	3	75
Totals	36	59.0	17	80.9

An explanation can be offered for the more active employment of the strict settlement in Northamptonshire. Once again it relates to the practice in Kent of settling only prospective jointure land in the life estate-entail manner without the implementation of trusts to preserve contingent remainders discussed above. A comparison of the percentages in Table 4 with Northamptonshire practice ill-ustrated in Table 5 demonstrates that landowners in both counties settling the bulk of their patrimonies at marriage employed the strict settlement with nearly equal frequency. In the main, the analysis of the marriage settlements in these two disparate counties highlights similarities in adoption rather than differences. We can therefore conclude with some confidence, albeit tentatively, that the strict settlement was adopted rather rapidly throughout the entire country.

19 A large quantity of settlements of Kentish yeoman survive. No example of a strict settlement appears until 1732: K.A.O. U1063/T45. This is the only surviving strict settlement executed in the period 1660–1740.
20 See above, fn. 16; including sequence no. 77 (a strict settlement of less than a manor).

To sum up, then, this enquiry into the adoption of the strict settlement demonstrates that the innovation was adopted rather rapidly by a broad segment of landed gentry in the counties under observation. Even by the 1680s, this form of conveyance was by far the most commonly employed type of marriage settlement for all segments of landed society, save for a minority of 'lesser gentry' who settled only prospective jointure land. It may therefore be concluded that knowledge of the device of trustees to preserve contingent remainders to protect settlements had reached both the London conveyancer with his battery of clients controlling great patrimonies and the country practitioner who settled the estates of lesser gentlemen before it appeared in the printed conveyancing books. Although we can only speculate as to the means by which such knowledge was disseminated, the most likely answer lies in the nature of the profession in early modern England, and its system of education and professional contacts. Regardless, our results do suggest that conveyancing was carried out by a body of practitioners who were highly responsive to advances in conveyancing technique, and that they were not reluctant to employ them before judicial sanction.

Finally the data cast doubt upon the assumptions of economic historians regarding the effect of the strict settlement, and in particular the nexus between its innovation and the 'rise of great estates'. That such a large proportion of each segment of landed society employed the device in an era when the various groups were alleged to have been experiencing differing economic fortunes tends to indicate that the strict settlement was rather a neutral factor. No doubt the settlement could preserve the patrimony of those members of landed society whose economic position was sound, but one wonders whether their estate actually required such protection.

6

MARRIAGE SETTLEMENTS IN PERSPECTIVE: THE SOCIAL AND ECONOMIC ASPECTS

In previous chapters the origins, judicial acceptance and dissemination of the strict settlement have been considered. Although the primary focus has been upon developments in the land law and its relationship to conveyancing practice, some inferences have been made concerning other matters, such as the nature of the legal profession and its receptivity to innovations in the mechanics of settlements.[1] But interest in the evolution of marriage settlements is not confined to matters of legal mechanics; nor is the device solely the province of the legal historian. During the later Middle Ages, the marriage settlement became a complex instrument dealing with intergenerational wealth transmission in the landed classes.[2] The substance of marriage settlements is therefore of interest to economic historians. But so too are the legal developments which have been considered, because they were bound to have had an effect upon landownership. Since they also dealt with wealth distribution within the family, the dispositions directed by marriage settlements are of concern to the social historian, family historian and historical sociologist. This chapter will deal with the socio-economic aspects of marriage settlements in the particular, and will also consider the speculations of historians regarding the motives which prompted conveyancers to devise a stricter form of settlement.

Some review of the historiography is in order, and it is appropriate to begin with the present assessment of the impact of the strict settlement upon landownership. The prevailing view, first put forward by Professor Sir John Habakkuk, is that there was an active land market after the Restoration, with a general drift of property in favour of the greater landowner during the period

1 See above, pp. 82–3, 91–2.
2 See above, pp. 1–10.

1680–1740.[3] Both the number of large proprietors and the relative
proportion of land under their control are said to have increased.
Primarily it was at the expense of the 'lesser gentry' and freeholders
that the agglomerations of the 'great magnates' were fashioned;
while the economic gap between the magnates and the 'substantial
squirearchy' widened, the estates of the latter survived the century
intact. The success of estate builders, however, was not due to the
greater efficiency of large units of ownership. Rather it was a
changing economic climate, and in particular the effects of the land
tax, which was undermining the position of the smaller landowner,
forcing him to part with property which his family might have held
for generations. Financed by the profits of office and the law, the
'great magnates' seized upon the opportunity to consolidate their
holdings by absorbing the estates of their lesser neighbours. Once
secured, they preserved their hegemony by employing strict family
settlements which prevented the dispersion of their estates by
their heirs.

In addition to preserving landed wealth, Professor Habakkuk
argues that the strict settlement actively promoted the accumulation of estates. Marriage, it is maintained, was the single most
important factor in the 'rise of great estates'; and due in part to the
widespread adoption of the strict settlement, acquisition through
marriage came to operate according to a fixed pattern. Regardless of
whether the bride was an heiress, she was required to make a
contribution towards enlarging her prospective husband's estate.
This contribution, the bride's portion, might take the form of land
or cash; if it was the latter, the marriage settlement often required
the purchase of estates which were to descend with the patrimony.
In the main, this process favoured the 'great magnates'; as
landowners with more substantial rent rolls could offer more
generous jointures, they commanded the brides with the largest

3 The thesis is first set out in 'English landownership 1680–1740', and further
developed in 'Marriage settlements in the eighteenth century'. The vital role
played by the strict settlement is also discussed in Professor Habakkuk's other
monographs on landowners and landownership in the late seventeenth and
eighteenth centuries: 'The long term rate of interest and the price of freehold land
in the seventeenth century', *Econ. Hist. Rev.*, 2nd ser. X (1952); 'Social attitudes
and attributes', in *The European nobility in the eighteenth century*, ed. A. Goodwin
(London, 1953); 'Daniel Finch, 2nd Earl of Nottingham: his house and estate', in
Studies in social history, ed. J. H. Plumb (London, 1955); 'The English
landmarket'; 'La disparition du paysan anglais', *Annales*, XX (1965); and
'Economic functions of English landowners in the seventeenth and eighteenth
century', in *Essays in agrarian history*, ed. W. E. Minchinton (London, 1968), 1.

portions. Since portions increased the size of the groom's family estate, the net effect became cumulative; that is to say, a successful match in one generation enhanced the family's bargaining position in the next.

While the application of portion money to the purchase of land contributed to the extension of the groom's patrimony, it did not necessarily precipitate an erosion of the bride's family estate. Although it might be necessary for the bride's father to mortgage part of his holdings in order to endow his daughter with a portion commensurate with the family's social position, it was only in extreme cases that he was forced to alienate. Professor Habakkuk concludes that, by allowing landowners to mortgage their own land to enlarge the estates of their sons-in-law, the landowning class was in effect 'raising itself up by its own bootstraps'.[4]

And there were heiresses; although fewer in number and thus overshadowed in effect by the numerous brides with large portions, the spectacular resuscitation in family fortune which a timely marriage to an heiress might engender rendered them a prized 'commodity'. Some demographic evidence exists to suggest that conditions were favourable for the production of heiresses. Dr Hollingsworth's calculations of the male generation replacement rates for the peerage indicates that the period 1680–1770 was a particularly severe one, with the male population of cohorts born between 1650 and 1725 not replacing themselves.[5] This demographic crisis may well have pervaded the entire landed class. If this was the case, a large number of heiresses would have been produced, especially since the patrimony was divided equally amongst surviving daughters. Again it was the 'great magnates' who benefited most according to Professor Habakkuk, attracting the best endowed of the landed heiresses with offers of large jointures; and again it was the marriage settlement which consolidated and preserved their acquisitions. Although the lands of an heiress might be settled upon her younger sons, a marriage might often produce only one surviving male child or the younger sons might die without male heirs. In both cases, the settlements would generally direct that the estate pass to the eldest son, thereby enlarging the patrimony.

4 Habakkuk, 'Marriage settlements', 28.
5 T. H. Hollingsworth, 'The demography of the British peerage', supplement to
   Population Studies, XVIII (1964), Table 21. Cf. Clay, 'Marriage, inheritance',
   517.

Finally, Professor Habakkuk maintains that the employment of the strict settlement established a more rational pattern of alienation in those families in which some retrenchment was required. Since the quality of legal estate held by the tenant in possession, a mere life interest, precluded an alienation in fee, the strict settlement ensured that land sales would take place only at the time of resettlement. The determination therefore had to be taken in concert with the eldest son, and perhaps with the bride's family; the adverse interests of the assembled parties would ensure that dispositions were kept to a minimum. Recourse to mortgages obviated the need for sporadic sales to meet sudden emergencies. Indeed, at the time of resettlement, families often opted for mortgaging rather than sale to satisfy their most pressing debts, thus postponing dispositions until the debt service exceeded the amount which could be spared from income.

Accordingly, it was in this fashion that the strict settlement contributed to the accumulation, as well as the preservation, of great estates. More recent enquiries into the land market in the eighteenth century, however, cast doubt upon some of Professor Habakkuk's generalizations. Both the soundness of his methodology and the logic, in economic terms, of his conclusions are called into question; and again the role of the strict settlement is very much in the forefront of the controversy. With regard to methodology, it is argued that Professor Habakkuk's reliance upon the land market in such 'untypical' counties as Northamptonshire and Bedfordshire to draw generalizations for the whole of England may well have been misplaced.[6] While disclaiming typicality for the region he has investigated, Dr J. V. Beckett concludes that Cumbria presents a contrast with Northamptonshire and Bedfordshire. Although he discounts the importance of the Habakkuk triad of marriage settlements, office holding and the land tax, Dr Beckett still discerns a general drift of landed property towards 'greater owners'. Therefore, in substance if not in form, movement in Cumbrian landownership is broadly similar to the pattern established in Northamptonshire and Bedfordshire; the period witnessed the building of larger estates.

Differences no doubt existed. In Cumbria, Dr Beckett finds that the successful families tended to be 'substantial squires' rather than

6 Beckett, 'English landownership', 567.

peers, but the lack of peerage interest in the region can be explained in part by the dearth of indigenous titled families. Moreover, as in Northamptonshire and Bedfordshire, the 'lesser gentry' were in decline; so too were the yeomanry, albeit 'marginally'. Thus, if we substitute 'great owners' for 'great magnates', we find that the general picture of Cumbrian landownership in large measure parallels the pattern in Northamptonshire and Bedfordshire: the concentration of property in fewer hands.

However, it is in Lincolnshire that developments in landownership present a more distinct contrast with the Habakkuk model.[7] Despite the widespread adoption of strict settlements and the operation of similar marriage patterns, Dr B. A. Holderness argues that the build-up of great estates at the expense of the lesser landowners was not a feature of eighteenth-century Lincolnshire. No oligarchy of either 'great owners' or 'great magnates' arose to dominate the land market in this county. Moreover, the gentry as a class held their own: although many families disappeared, they were replaced by landowners of similar stature. Yet the land market in Lincolnshire also had its peculiarities. Dr Holderness considers the activity of local farmers in the land market to be of paramount importance, accounting in large measure for the predominance during the century of small transactions. In addition, a rather large number of absentee landowners, not a factor present for the most part in Northamptonshire, Bedfordshire and Cumbria, also affected the land market.

Thus the similarities and differences illustrated by the various local studies of the land market demonstrate, as Dr Beckett aptly suggests, 'the hazards of generalizing from the particular'.[8] And the rather uniform employment of strict settlements in counties with differing trends in landownership tends to undermine Professor Habakkuk's nexus between marriage settlements and the 'rise of great estates'. In addition, some doubts are raised as to whether there was actually a decline in the volume of land sales after mid-century, a development which Professor Habakkuk attributes in part to the widespread adoption of strict settlements. Again the attack is methodological: both Professor F. M. L. Thompson and Dr Christopher Clay question Professor Habakkuk's reliance upon the decreased incidence of estate acts and final concords to

7 Holderness, 'The English land market'.
8 Beckett, 'English landownership', 581.

demonstrate a static land market.[9] In countering Professor Habakkuk's literary evidence regarding a dearth of land on the market, Dr Clay finds no evidence of a shortage of land in the correspondence of those families which he has investigated who were interested in building or consolidating their estates. While conceding the upward movement in the price of land over the century cited by Professor Habakkuk as evidence for a dwindling supply of land, Dr Clay demonstrates that it was sporadic, and linked to fluctuations in the price of government securities. Consequently, rises in purchase rates paralleled periods when the national debt did not expand; conversely in war time, with increases in public borrowing and concomitant rises in interest rates, the funds became a more attractive investment with a corresponding slackening in demand for land. According to Dr Clay, therefore, it was increased demand for land rather than shrinking supply which affected land prices during the period.

Thus the Habakkuk model, and therefore the nexus between the strict settlement and 'the rise of great estates', has come under some rather severe methodological criticism. But perhaps more significantly the logic of Professor Habakkuk's economic conclusions concerning the relationship between marriage and inheritance and the 'rise of great estates' has also been challenged. In questioning whether the 'great magnates' actually benefited more than the other segments of landed society from the workings of marriage and inheritance, Dr Clay stresses the strong element of chance in determining whether the estate of the potential heiress actually devolved with the patrimony.[10] Demographic accidents such as the groom's death before the birth of a male heir might result in the loss of her estate, while at the same time charging the patrimony with the hefty jointure which had been offered to secure her inheritance. On the other hand, an untimely death could create an heiress after her marriage, enlarging her husband's patrimony at

9 F. M. L. Thompson, 'Landownership and economic growth in England in the eighteenth century', in *Agrarian change and economic development*, ed. E. J. Jones and S. L. Woolf (London, 1970); and Christopher Clay, 'The price of freehold land in the later seventeenth and eighteenth century', *Econ. Hist Rev.*, 2nd ser. XXVII (1974). Professor Thompson suggests that other forms of sale, such as auctions, may account for the decreased incidence of fines. Dr Clay disputes some of Professor Habakkuk's calculations and contends that our knowledge of eighteenth-century conveyancing practice is insufficient for us to conclude that a decrease in the number of fines demonstrates a decrease in land transfers.
10 Clay, 'Marriage and inheritance', 505–9.

no great expense in the way of her jointure. Disappointment and windfalls were not uncommon in a society so much at the mercy of misfortunes in mortality. As the 'great magnates' were no more immune from these demographic quirks than their lesser neighbours, Dr Clay contends that the effects of marriage and inheritance should fall impartially upon all segments of landed society.

Moreover, Dr Clay questions the economic benefit derived by the landed class as a whole in mortgaging to raise portions, even where the sum was expended in enlarging the groom's estate. Because the rate of interest on mortgages during the period exceeded the yield on land, the process was actually reducing the net income of the landed class. According to Dr Clay, the landed class, far from 'pulling itself up by its bootstraps', was actually being drained by this cycle, in an era when relatively static rents were insufficient to compensate for increased debt service.[11]

Regardless of whether the 'bootstraps' argument is a specious one, there is in fact little evidence to suggest that portions were actually expended on the acquisition of land. Recent family studies indicate that portion money was often used to meet pressing obligations rather than to enlarge the patrimony; and an analysis of the marriage settlements which comprise the data set confirms that only in rare instances was it stipulated that the portion be used to buy land. For example, Thomas Coke, later first Earl of Leicester, used £10,000 of his bride's £15,000 portion to satisfy his sisters' portions which were a charge upon his Norfolk estates pursuant to his father's will; no evidence exists to suggest that the residue was expended on land.[12] Likewise, the Duke of Newcastle used his bride's portion to discharge mortgages on his Sussex estate.[13] Not one of the marriage settlements of the Cowpers or the Grimstones stipulated that the portion money be spent on land acquisition.[14] Indeed, in our group of 104 post-1660 Kentish marriage settlements, only eight contain provisions for disposing of the portion money.[15] Two[16] of the eight settlements were upon younger sons,

11 *Ibid.*, 507.
12 R. A. C. Parker, *Code of Norfolk: a financial and agricultural study 1702–1842* (Oxford, 1975), 12.
13 Kelch, *Newcastle*, 44–7.
14 Clay, thesis, 422.
15 Sequence nos. 56, 73, 103, 120, 130, 135, 140, 143.
16 Sequence nos. 73, 103.

while three[17] were of urban or 'pseudo-gentry'. Thus in only three marriage settlements was the portion money stipulated to be expended to enlarge an *existing* patrimony.[18] Similarly, only five of the forty-one Northamptonshire settlements executed after 1660 earmark the portion for land purchase.[19] Three were settlements upon younger sons, while another was to increase the patrimony of a London merchant.[20] Only in one settlement, upon the marriage of Francis Raynesford, Esquire, was the portion directed to be spent on land to increase the patrimony of a landed squire.[21]

Although the failure to specify that portion money be expended on land does not prove conclusively that it was spent otherwise, it does suggest that the groom and his family had a free hand. The Earl of Leicester and the Duke of Newcastle were not alone in the need for the ready cash that a portion provided. In 1706, Edward Filmer, son and heir of Sir Robert Filmer of East Sutton, Baronet, married Mary Wallis, the daughter of an Oxfordshire squire. Mary brought with her a portion of £5,000. According to the pre-nuptial Articles of Agreement, £1,000 came directly into the hands of Sir Robert upon the solemnization of the marriage to do with as he pleased, while the remaining £4,000 was to be vested in trustees.[22] Under the terms of a trust, a sum was to be raised to discharge the estate of portions provided by the will of Sir Robert's father.[23] It would therefore appear that instead of being expended to enlarge the patrimony, portions were more commonly used to discharge present obligations, save in cases where a new branch of a landed family was being spawned.

Finally, Dr Clay employs the Hollingsworth data to suggest an explanation for the more stable land market in the second half of the eighteenth century.[24] For various reasons, failure of male issue was a frequent cause of land coming on to the market. Often, for example, a collateral inheritance was heavily charged with legacies for daughters, or else distant from the collateral heir's estate;

17 Sequence nos. 120, 135, 143.
18 Sequence nos. 56, 130, 140.
19 Sequence nos. 261, 262, 270, 272, 280.
20 Sequence nos. 261, 262, 270, 280.
21 Sequence no. 272.
22 K.A.O. U120 T125.
23 K.A.O. U120 T200/16. Sir Robert, 2nd Baronet, left portions of £2,000 for each of his three daughters.
24 Clay, 'Marriage, inheritance', 515–18.

therefore it might be more prudent to sell it and reinvest the proceeds elsewhere. Consequently, the increased production of males in the second quarter of the eighteenth century would decrease the incidence of land passing to collateral heirs, thereby reducing the quantity of land coming on to the market for this reason.

In addition to these objections, our enquiry into the dissemination of the strict settlement also casts some doubts upon the Habakkuk nexus.[25] It has been argued that the 'great magnates' employed the strict settlement earlier than their lesser neighbours and entailed more of their estate. While our data have not allowed us to test the latter proposition, it has been demonstrated that a large segment of the allegedly declining 'lesser gentry' frequently employed strict settlements of a considerable portion of their estates. If, other things being equal, the strict settlement was the principal factor in establishing the primacy of the 'great magnates' and the survival of the 'substantial squirearchy', one would expect the strict settlement to have prevented the dispersion of their estates as well.

Finally, the Habakkuk thesis ignores certain demographic factors crucial to the operation of the strict settlement in the manner suggested. The effect of a single strict settlement executed upon marriage was to insure that the male heir produced by the marriage would succeed to the estate intact. Stated more simply, it restrained powers of alienation for one generation: the groom became a life tenant and the trustees to preserve contingent remainders prevented him from alienating any settled land for longer than his own life. A single strict settlement, then, operated as a bridle for one lifetime. The eldest son upon his father's death came into possession as a tenant in tail with full powers of disposition. It is thus unlikely that a single strict settlement would have had the long-term preservative effect that Professor Habakkuk suggests.

In practice, however, restraint could be maintained if resettlement occurred before the death of the life tenant. The procedure for resettlement required that a second strict settlement be executed, and in practice this occurred upon the marriage of the eldest son. The procedure was as follows: father and son join in a settlement in which the son relinquishes his entail in remainder and accepts

---

25 See above, pp. 87–92.

instead a life estate to commence upon the determination of his father's life interest. In order to prompt his son to make such a sacrifice, the father settles some form of present income upon the son to support his household until he comes into possession of the estate. The existing settlement is therefore broken, and replaced with one which spans a further generation.

It is therefore a pattern of successive resettlements which affords the continuity in landownership crucial to the Habakkuk nexus. But for the strict settlement to operate in this fashion presupposes the existence of a demographic climate which is dubious given the limited life expectancy, late age of marriage and high child mortality which characterized early modern England: that fathers actually survive to the marriage of their eldest sons. Elsewhere, a model of intergenerational succession required for the effective operation of the strict settlement has been constructed and was tested against the demographic realities of England in the late seventeenth and early eighteenth centuries.[26] The results suggest that in only about one succession in three did a father actually survive to resettle the patrimony at the marriage of his eldest son.

Research by a number of economic historians, as well as our own enquiry into the dissemination of the strict settlement, therefore casts considerable doubt upon the Habakkuk nexus between the strict settlement and the 'rise of great estates'. But the link between the development of the strict settlement and the economic fortunes of the landed class in the late seventeenth and early eighteenth centuries is not confined to estate building and preservation: it has been suggested that the innovation had a profound impact upon provision for younger sons and daughters.[27] Indeed, Sir William Blackstone wrote that the design of the developers of the strict settlement was 'to secure in family settlements a provision for the future children of an intended marriage, who before were usually left at the mercy of the particular tenant for life'.[28]

Although not embracing this view, Professor Habakkuk argues that both the legal mechanics and the actual form which provisions

---

26 Lloyd Bonfield, 'Marriage settlements and the "rise of great estates": the demographic aspect', *Econ. Hist. Rev.*, 2nd ser. XXXII (1979). For a comment on the model, see B. English and J. Saville, 'Family settlements and the "rise of great estates"' and my reply in *Econ. Hist. Rev.*, 2nd ser. XXXIII (1980).
27 Habakkuk, 'Marriage settlements', 15–16.
28 2 *Bl. Comm.*, 172.

for younger sons and daughters assumed varied greatly in the eighteenth century from those previously employed.[29] Essentially Professor Habakkuk has discerned two fundamental changes. In the first place, he maintains that it was less customary in the earlier period for provisions for younger sons and daughters to be specified in the marriage settlement. Consequently, the decision regarding the amount of provision was left to the discretion of the parent at the appropriate time, upon a daughter's marriage or a son's majority. To some extent, this method of provision was preferable to a binding commitment entered into upon marriage, since a father could assess his financial position at the appropriate time and provide accordingly. From the standpoint of the daughters and younger sons, however, there was a significant drawback. Since provisions were an item of family expenditure which might painlessly be diminished, there was a danger that some fathers might heed the advice of Lord Delamer, and seek to economize at the expense of their 'excess children': 'To provide convenient matches for your daughters if you can, is without doubt your Duty, as also to give them good portions, but not such as will make your eldest sonne uneasy, for that is to give them more than comes to their share.'[30] Secondly, Habakkuk contends that the substance of provisions for younger sons was transformed over the period, and that fathers were less generous towards them than towards their daughters. It is maintained that, in the earlier period, provisions for younger sons took the form of estates carved out of the patrimony, while later cash sums were directed. The amount, however, was less substantial than that bestowed upon daughters.

While the transformation in the form of provision described by Professor Habakkuk tended to keep the patrimony intact, the change placed a substantial burden on the estate to raise the requisite capital sums. While thrifty landowners might save portions out of income, others were no doubt forced to take advantage of the limited powers of mortgage which were written into most settlements. Over a number of generations, successive mortgaging would have led to serious indebtedness with an increasing portion of estate income devoted to debt service. Eventually, either retrenchment or land sales must have followed;

29 Habakkuk, 'Marriage settlements', 15–16.
30 *The works of the Right Honourable Henry late Lord Delamer* (London, 1694), 33.

and historians have considered the middle of the eighteenth century as the crucial period.[31] But if the strict settlement was adopted in the 1660s, one must wonder why it took nearly a century, four or five generations, for the burden to become intolerable. An investigation into the legal form employed may resolve this dilemma, as well as test Blackstone's suppositions regarding the motives of the developers of the strict settlement. The family muniments exploited in previous chapters provide a data base to investigate these matters, and the appropriate time to begin is the turn of the seventeenth century.

Relatively few of the early-seventeenth-century marriage settlements which comprise the data set contain provisions for the younger sons and daughters which might be produced by the impending marriage. Furthermore, the legal mechanics employed in most of these settlements rendered the payment of the prescribed portions dependent either upon the discretion of the tenant in possession or upon the demographic situation of the family. In only two settlements, both provisions for daughters' portions, was the sum forthcoming regardless of these factors.[32] It would appear therefore that Professor Habakkuk's contention that the early-seventeenth-century marriage settlement was not the vehicle for provisions for younger sons and daughters is substantially correct. Ultimately the onus must have fallen upon the parents to determine both the amount and the form of provisions at the appropriate time. In practice, however, mortality rates dictated that many of these decisions would in fact be prospective, since a substantial proportion of fathers must not have lived to the marriage of their daughters or the majority of their younger sons.[33] In such cases, it was likely that the will served as the vehicle for provision. An example of

31 Mingay, *English landed society*, 35–6. Portions were, of course, not the only source of indebtedness. See David Cannadine, 'Aristocratic indebtedness in the nineteenth century: the case re-opened', *Econ. Hist. Rev.*, 2nd ser. XXX (1977), 627–8; 638–44.
32 Sequence nos. 35, 39. In my data set eighty-four settlements, sequence nos. 1–45 and 201–39, were executed during the period 1601–59. Of these, twenty (23.8%) contain some type of provision for daughters and/or younger sons: sequence nos. 1, 3, 21, 23, 35, 39, 201, 214, 215, 216, 220, 221, 222, 224, 229, 233, 235, 236, 238, 239.
33 In Bonfield, 'Marriage settlements and the "rise of great estates"', I argued that only about one-third of peerage fathers survived to the marriage of their eldest sons. Admittedly more would probably have survived to marry off their daughters, since women married at a younger age: T. H. Hollingsworth, 'Demography of the British peerage', supplement to *Population Studies*, XVIII

early-seventeenth-century practice can be provided by examining the records of the Filmers of East Sutton, Kentish baronets. Both Sir Edward and his heir, Sir Robert, directed in their wills that the profits of the rectory of East Sutton which had not been placed under settlement at marriage should be used to raise portions for their younger sons and daughters.[34]

Some families did attempt to furnish portions for prospective younger sons and daughters by marriage settlement, despite the fact that the provisions would be avoided if the eldest son alienated or resettled the patrimony. Basically, three forms were employed to secure the provisions. The first was for the settlor to grant or reserve a power to charge the estate with portions or annuities. The second method was to render the enjoyment of a gift over conditional upon the remainderman furnishing a prescribed portion; and finally, the settlor could create a trust to receive the profits from a segment of the patrimony to raise a specified sum.

Turning to the first method of provisions, the limitation of a power of appointment to the life tenant to allow him by deed or will to grant an annuity or capital sum in favour of his younger sons or daughters, an example can be furnished from the settlements of the Tuftons of Hothfield, Earls of Thanet. In the marriage settlement of his eldest son, Nicholas (later first Earl of Thanet), executed in 1602, Sir John Tufton, Baronet, empowered his son to grant annuities of one hundred marks to each of Nicholas's prospective younger sons and forty marks to each prospective daughter out of the settled estates.[35] Sir John also undertook to provide his granddaughters with portions, but only if his son predeceased him leaving no male issue.

By contrast, Sir John's arrangements for his own younger sons and daughters were far more complex. In March 1603, Sir John provided for his four younger sons and three daughters by settling outlying estates upon them.[36] Later the estates limited to his

(1964), Table 17. Moreover, in about one-half of the families a daughter would have been the first child produced. As for younger sons, some would reach majority, usually considered age 18 in settlements, before their elder brothers married. Once again more fathers would have survived to provide for their younger sons. Still the overall demographic climate indicates that many fathers would have died before providing for their children.

34 K.A.O. U120 T200/10 (1629); K.A.O. U120 T200/14 (1651).
35 Sequence no. 1.
36 K.A.O. U455 T280/1.

daughters were revoked in favour of cash portions.[37] Sir John then executed a further conveyance of these estates to his own use for life with remainder to his eldest son in tail, but reserving the power to appoint up to two-thirds of the premises for twenty-one years to discharge his debts and legacies.[38] By the time of his death in 1624, Sir John had already provided an additional £4,000 to three of his four sons, and in fact charged the estate with only a number of small legacies.[39] Thus, four documents were required for Sir John to provide for his younger sons and daughters, while his eldest son need only execute one.

Upon the marriage of his eldest son in 1629, Nicholas, now the first Earl of Thanet, executed a resettlement of the Tufton patrimony.[40] The pattern established a generation before was once again employed. Since the resettlement revoked the power of appointment which his father had limited in him, it was necessary for the Earl to reserve a similar right; and in fact both the Earl and his eldest son, John, were allowed the option of appointing the profits of a segment of the patrimony for twenty-one years. However, in this settlement, neither the form nor the amount of the provision was prescribed; and, more significantly, no provision was made for daughters. When the first Earl died in 1631, he appointed an annuity of £200 to his younger son Cecil, who was a minor.[41] To provide portions of £3,000 for each of his two daughters, he directed his executor to charge the manors of Dingmarsh and Westwell Park which had remained unsettled.

Thus by reserving powers of appointment in their marriage settlements, and by charging land which remained unsettled by will, the Tuftons provided portions for their younger sons and daughters. Other families followed the same course.[42] But whether the portions were in fact granted was at the discretion of the father;

---

37 *Ibid.*, the revocation was attested on the reverse of the settlement, but the amounts of the portions were not recorded.
38 K.A.O. U455 T280/1.
39 P.R.O. PROB 11/114, fo. 29. An additional £300 was left to his second son, Humphrey, while Richard and William received £150 each. William Tufton was to receive an additional £1,000 if he executed a release of all right and title to land in which he might have a claim in gavelkind. A settlement of land upon his second son, Sir Humphrey, Knight, remains amongst the family muniments, K.A.O. U455 T280/2.
40 Sequence no. 23.
41 P.R.O. PROB 11/160, fo. 119.
42 Sequence nos. 216, 220, 221, 222, 224, 235.

the children had no legal claim to their portions under the settlement. In the second method of provision employed by Kentish families before 1660, the children did have legal claims to portions, but by its terms the portion was to be paid only under certain conditions.[43] In each case, it was the ultimate remainder-man, that is to say the collateral male heir rather than the eldest son produced by the marriage, who was required to pay the portion in order to come into enjoyment of his interest.[44] Consequently, a daughter was assured of a portion only if she had no brothers.

One of the families whose marriage settlement is included in our data set did, however, annex a condition to pay portions upon the enjoyment of the entail by the eldest son produced by the marriage. In 1601, John Cope of Canons Ashby, a Northamptonshire squire, executed a post-nuptial settlement upon the marriage of his eldest son and heir, Erasmus, with Mary Throckmorton.[45] The settlement was a complex one, containing a two-fold disposition of the patrimony. Cope retained a life interest in both segments, and after his death a trust was limited for six months to raise money to pay his debts and legacies. Upon the termination of the trust, the manor of Canons Ashby was settled upon his wife as jointure, followed by an entail male in Erasmus. Upon Cope's death and the expiration of the term in his executors, the capital messuage of Eidon, along with various lands and tenements in Northamptonshire, was limited to Erasmus for life and upon his death to Mary as jointure. A remainder to the heirs male of Erasmus was conditional upon the payment of £2,000 to provide portions for daughters produced by the marriage.

This rather unique method for a settlor to provide prospectively for portions for daughters produced by the marriage was relatively secure. Once the contingent entail vested, upon the death of Erasmus, the daughters produced by the marriage had an enforceable right to their portions. Should no male child survive, the collateral male heir would also be required to furnish the portions. There was, however, one snag: during his lifetime, Erasmus could defeat the intention of his father to provide portions for the

43 Sequence nos. 3, 23.
44 The form of the settlement was: 'To groom for life, then to bride as jointure, remainder to the heirs male of their bodies, remainder to the heirs of groom if they pay the sum of £X to the daughters produced by the marriage, in default to daughters in common, remainder to the right heirs of groom.'
45 Sequence no. 201.

daughters produced by the marriage either by alienating Eidon or by resettling the estate.

The final method of provision by marriage settlement involved the creation of a trust.[46] Various mechanical forms were employed, but in most cases whether the trust came into operation depended upon the demographic situation of the family. The mechanics of the settlement ran as follows:

> to groom for life, then to bride as jointure, remainder to the heirs male of the body of groom on the body of bride and for default of issue to trustees for X years to raise portions for the daughters of groom and bride, upon the determination of the trust to the heirs male of groom.

While the daughters produced by the marriage had an enforceable right to their prescribed portions, the trust came into operation only if the marriage produced no male child. In substance, then, this type of provision was similar to the one in which the remainder over to the collateral male heir was conditioned upon the payment of a portion.

Thus provisions for younger sons and daughters in the settlements which comprise our data set were conditioned upon family demography or the good-will of the tenant in possession. There were, however, two exceptions. Upon his own marriage in 1642, Christopher Lord Teynham limited a portion of the patrimony in trust for a term of 1,000 years which was to commence immediately, in order to raise the sum of £6,000 to be divided equally amongst the daughters produced by his impending marriage.[47] After the sum was raised, the trust was to cease, and the reversion was granted to his heir male. No similar arrangement was made for his younger sons. Similarly, Sir John Baker, Baronet, employed a trust to provide for prospective daughters in a settlement upon the marriage of his eldest son with the daughter of Robert Newton, Esquire.[48] However, in this case the trust was less secure; unlike the one employed by Lord Teynham, the trustees in the Baker settlement did not come into immediate enjoyment of a part of the patrimony. In the marriage settlement, Sir John effected a three-part disposition of his estates, and the trust commenced upon the determination of different estates depending upon the segment: after his

46 Sequence nos. 214, 215, 220, 235, 236, 238, 239.
47 Sequence no. 214.
48 Sequence no. 39.

wife's jointure; after his son's life estate; and after his daughter-in-law's jointure. Until a daughter was born, however, the second and third trusts might be destroyed by the connivance of Sir John's male heir. Consequently, by the mid-seventeenth century, the time when the strict settlement was developed, portions were not generally directed prospectively by marriage settlement. In those settlements which did include provisions, the enjoyment of the portion was conditional upon family demography or fatherly discretion. Clearly, the marriage settlement was destined to become the vehicle for raising portions, but the issue which Blackstone's observation raises is whether the development of the mechanics of the strict settlement and the widespread use of the marriage settlement to appoint secure portions was simultaneous. In order to determine this point, the period from 1660 (the date when strict settlements appear in the data set) to 1740 has been divided into twenty-year intervals, and the manner of provision by settlement in each interval will be determined.

In the first two decades which witnessed the adoption of strict settlements in Kent and Northamptonshire (1660–80), twenty-six of the marriage settlements which comprise the data set employed this form.[49] Of these twenty-six strict settlements, twenty contained no provisions for daughters and younger sons, about three-quarters (76.9%),[50] while in none of the fifteen 'non-strict' marriage settlements were portions stipulated. The number of strict settlements directing provisions for daughters and younger sons presents a striking contrast with the pattern which has been established for the previous sixty years, when less than a quarter of the settlements executed contained provisions for daughters and younger sons. To some extent, these bare figures tend to substantiate Blackstone's conclusion that the development of the strict settlement should be attributed to the demands of settlors for a more secure method of providing for their younger sons and daughters. Before reaching any firm conclusions, however, further investigation must be undertaken of the forms which these provisions assumed.

The legal mechanics to secure provisions for daughters

49 Sequence nos. 46, 51, 54, 56, 57, 61, 62, 63, 64, 67, 68, 69, 72, 241, 242, 243, 244, 245, 246, 247, 248, 249, 250, 251, 252, 253.
50 Sequence nos. 46, 51, 56, 57, 61, 62, 64, 67, 69, 241, 242, 243, 244, 245, 246, 247, 248, 249, 250, 251.

employed by settlors executing strict settlements were not novel. Conveyancers actually adopted a form of provision which was in use in the earlier part of the seventeenth century, the limitation of a term in trust after the entail limited to the eldest son produced by the marriage. But it has been noted that this settlement did not unconditionally assure daughters of their portions; whether they received the prescribed sum depended upon the demographic situation of the family.

Initially, then, the advent of the strict settlement did not radically alter the legal mechanics by which settlors provided portions for their daughters. Moreover, the adoption of the strict settlement did not enhance the prospects for daughters actually receiving their portion. The early form of strict settlement merely employed the mechanics developed during the first half of the seventeenth century. Admittedly, some security was offered, because the estate in the trustees to preserve contingent remainders prevented the life tenant from defeating the interest in the trustees to raise portions. But the trust to raise portions came into effect only if no surviving male child was produced; consequently a daughter was assured of a portion only if she had no surviving brothers.

Thus the form to provide portions for daughters employed in strict settlements was similar to the one adopted by settlors in many 'pre-strict' settlements. Moreover, the mechanics were in substance no different from annexing a condition to pay portions to daughters to the limitation in fee in the collateral remainderman; indeed this form was not entirely abandoned.[51] Admittedly this earlier method was less sophisticated, but it was also less cumbersome. No trustees were required to receive the profits, and the collateral male heir came into enjoyment of the patrimony immediately. To satisfy the portions, he could mortgage the estate, since the ultimate remainder was generally in fee. There were, however, advantages to the 'trust' method in that it offered the daughters more protection, since trusts were enforceable in Chancery, a forum more inclined to protect the interests of women.[52] Moreover, the trustees were often related to the settlor or his close friends, and therefore took a personal interest in the welfare of the daughters. In addition, the trustees were often empowered to raise a

---

51 Sequence no. 51.
52 Cioni, thesis, conclusion.

specified sum for the maintenance of the daughters until the portions became payable.[53] Finally, to allow the remainderman to come into enjoyment of the estate immediately, settlors often provided a right of entry if the remainderman 'put in security' to pay the portions.[54]

While the 'trust' was the most commonly employed method of providing for daughters, the grant or reservation of a power of appointment to charge the settled estate with capital sums and annuities continued to be employed.[55] In one case, a groom reserved the power to appoint portions for his daughters only if he had no male heirs,[56] while in other cases the discretionary power to appoint portions for daughters and annuities for younger sons was coupled with the 'trust' provision should the settlor's son produce no male heirs.[57]

Thus in the first two decades of the employment of the strict settlement in Kent and Northamptonshire, there was little change in either the legal mechanics or the prospects for daughters to receive a portion by marriage settlement. The interposing of the limitation in trustees to preserve contingent remainders merely protected the settlement. Whether the daughters actually received their portions depended upon demographic factors: was there a surviving male heir to come into possession of the patrimony? If so, the portions prescribed in the marriage settlement were not forthcoming. If fathers with sons wished to provide portions for their daughters or younger sons, it was imperative to allow a portion of the patrimony to remain unsettled so that they might charge this segment with legacies to provide their children with portions.

Turning now to the second twenty-year period (1681–1700) following the development of the strict settlement, twenty-three of the twenty-nine strict settlements (79.3%) contain provisions for prospective younger sons and daughters.[58] The pattern which emerges over these two decades is similar to the one established for

53 Sequence nos. 57, 61, 67, 248.
54 Sequence nos. 62, 64, 67, 245, 248, 249. Invariably, maximum sums were appointed to be equally divided amongst surviving children. Thus it was necessary for the next remainderman to bind himself to pay this amount.
55 Sequence nos. 46, 67, 242, 250, 251.
56 Sequence no. 46.
57 Sequence nos. 67, 242, 250, 251.
58 Sequence nos. 75, 76, 81, 82, 86, 88, 89, 90, 91, 92, 94, 95, 96, 255, 256, 257, 258, 259, 260, 261, 262, 263, 264.

the previous period; it does, however, witness the adoption of two other forms of provision. Still, the most common manner of providing for daughters' portions remained the limitation of term in trust in all or part of the patrimony following the remainder to the eldest son, but preceding the limitation to the settlor's right heir.[59] Discretionary powers to charge the estate with portions for daughters and younger sons were reserved by five settlors, and this was the second most common method of provision.[60] But it must be stressed that the father was under no obligation to appoint the portions, and the children therefore had no recourse in the courts.

During this period, the last two decades of the seventeenth century, two novel forms were employed. In two of the settlements which are included in the data set, provisions for daughters were directed if the bride predeceased her husband without leaving male issue.[61] While these provisions were legally enforceable, the daughters were in a similar position to those provided by the 'trust'; that is, daughters only profited if no son was produced. Therefore, it was only in collateral inheritances that the portion was a charge upon the estate.

To provide portions for daughters and younger sons regardless of whether a son was produced, a variation of the 'trust' manner of provision was developed and employed by two of our settlors.[62] The legal mechanics adopted were again quite simple: in addition to the term limited in trust after the remainder to the eldest son produced by the marriage, another term was limited to the same trustees which took effect upon determination of the estate in jointure limited to the widow. Thus the term in trust commenced *before* the eldest son came into possession of the patrimony. Consequently, the first trust to raise portions took effect regardless of whether the marriage produced a male heir. Under these settlements, the younger sons and daughters had legally enforceable provisions regardless of the family's demographic or economic position.

Two points regarding the adoption of this 'two-pronged' trust are

59 Sequence nos. 81, 91, 94, 95, 96, 255, 256, 257, 258, 259, 260, 261, 262, 263, 264.
60 Sequence nos. 82, 86, 90, 92, 262.
61 Sequence nos. 88, 89.
62 Sequence nos. 75, 76. The settlors were Sir Robert Filmer, Baronet, settling his estate in 1682 upon the marriage of his eldest son with Elizabeth, daughter and co-heir of Sir William Beversham, Knight, one of the Masters in Chancery; and William Courthope, Esquire, who executed a marriage settlement in 1682 upon the marriage of his heir with Anne Godfrey.

worthy of note. In the first place, both settlors employing this form directed that the sum raised by the first term be *equally* divided amongst the younger sons and daughters; until the portions were dispersed, at the age of twenty-one for younger sons and at the time of marriage for daughters, the interest upon the capital sum to be raised was to be expended to provide education and maintenance for the children. Daughters received a larger endowment only if there was no male heir, and thus no younger sons, for then the second trust was to come into operation to increase the portions of the surviving daughters. Secondly, since the trustees were to come into immediate possession upon the determination of the jointure estate in the widow, it was imperative that a clause be inserted to allow the heir male to come into possession if he 'put in security' to pay the prescribed portions. The intent of the settlor in employing this form was not to prevent his eldest son from coming into enjoyment of the patrimony, but to insure that he would undertake to provide the prescribed portions.

The turn of the eighteenth century witnessed a slight decrease in the number of settlors providing for their younger sons and daughters by marriage settlement. Nineteen of the twenty-six settlors, again about three-quarters (73.1%) of those who executed strict settlements in the first two decades of the eighteenth century, made provisions for prospective younger sons and daughters.[63] Only one employed a form other than the 'trust'.[64] Moreover, the 'two-pronged' trust employed by the Filmers and the Courthopes a generation earlier began to emerge as the most common form of provision in Kent. In six of the Kentish strict settlements, all or part of the patrimony was limited to trustees for a term of years to raise portions for younger sons and daughters which preceded the remainder in tail to the eldest son; after the entail, a second term was limited to trustees to increase the portions of the surviving daughters.[65] During the period a second form of provision for younger sons and daughters appeared; one of our settlors merely employed the 'first prong' of the 'two-pronged' trust, by limiting a

63 Sequence nos. 100, 101, 103, 107, 108, 111, 114, 116, 120, 121, 122, 265, 266, 267, 268, 269, 270, 271.
64 Of the settlements listed in fn. 63 above, only sequence no. 120 did not employ a trust. The provision there was that if the bride died without male issue, but with surviving daughters, the daughters were to come into possession of the estate as tenants in common unless the groom or his heirs paid a portion of £1,000.
65 Sequence nos. 101, 105, 108, 111, 121, 122.

term in trust to raise portions for younger sons and daughters before granting the remainder in tail to the eldest son produced by the marriage.[66]

In contrast, Northamptonshire settlors during the period do not appear to have adopted the 'two pronged' trust as actively. Of the seven strict settlements employing trusts to provide for younger sons and daughters only one employed the 'two-pronged' trust.[67] The majority of the Northamptonshire families whose settlements are included in the data set continued to provide portions for daughters only if the impending marriage produced no surviving male child.

With the increased incidence of trusts to raise portions for daughters and younger sons, there was a commensurate decline in the employment of other methods of securing portions. The limitation of the gift over to the ultimate remainderman conditional upon the payment of a specified portion to daughters disappeared altogether, while only three settlements granted a discretionary power to appoint portions.[68]

Thus in Kent it was the first two decades of the eighteenth century that witnessed the widespread appearance of a form of strict settlement which provided for legally enforceable portions for younger sons and daughters regardless of the demographic situation of the family. No longer was failure of male issue necessary to charge the estate with portions. During the final two decades under consideration, there was an increased incidence of terms limited to trustees in this manner, and the practice also became common in Northamptonshire. Nine of the twenty settlements contain provisions for the 'two-pronged' trust,[69] while seven contain limitations to trustees to raise portions for younger sons and daughters before the remainder in tail to the eldest son.[70] Of the remaining four settlements, three provide trusts to raise portions for daughters only if no son was produced,[71] while the remaining settlement reserves a power of appointment.[72] A power of appointment also appears in one of the 'trust' provisions, to allow the father the

66 Sequence no. 114.
67 Sequence no. 268.
68 Sequence nos. 120, 269, 271.
69 Sequence nos. 130, 131, 136, 139, 141, 272, 274, 275, 277.
70 Sequence nos. 129, 135, 140, 146, 273, 279, 280.
71 Sequence nos. 126, 132, 142.
72 Sequence no. 127.

discretion of appointing portions for his daughters if an heir male was produced.[73]

Having dated the transformation in the pattern of provisions for younger sons and daughters from discretionary to mandatory, the economic significance of the change may be assessed. Essentially, the concern will be to note its financial implications. In the initial pattern employed in the forty years after the development of strict settlement the term limited in trust to raise portions came into operation only in a generation in which no eldest son was produced; thus the portions which were mandated in the settlements became a charge upon the estate only in collateral inheritances. Accordingly, in families where there was an unbroken 'chain of succession' from father to son, portions still remained discretionary; and if the father desired to endow his children, the sum would have to be raised from unsettled land. Perhaps at the time of resettlement, if one did occur, the father and his eldest son might determine in concert the amount and the source of the provisions for the groom's brothers and sisters, bearing in mind the economic circumstances of the family.

However, after the turn of the century no such process would occur with the majority of our landowners, because the form of strict settlement employed charged the estate with portions *before* the grant of the remainder in tail to the eldest son. Portions, therefore, were a charge upon the estate regardless upon whom the patrimony descended. Thus it was only in the later period that in *each generation* where a younger son or daughter was produced the estate was required to bear the burden of portions: amounts which had been fixed a generation earlier, and which were legally enforceable by the trustees. Under the prevailing manner of provision in the later period, there was no alternative but to meet this obligation regardless of the family's economic circumstances. Often it might be necessary to mortgage; but for most families the burden of debt would not have become pressing until mid-century, after two or three generations of strict settlements employing this form of trust were executed. Since it was the upper stratum of landed society which employed this form most frequently, their estates must have been more vulnerable.

Could the landed class afford to be so generous to its 'excess children'? Unfortunately, no precise answer can be offered for landed society as a whole, or even for the body of landowners whose marriage settlements are included in the data set. Their generosity no doubt varied, and perhaps not in proportion to financial means. Moreover, the value of the estates placed under strict settlement often cannot be gleaned from the conveyances. In the main, the settlements recite a description of each parcel conveyed, rather than the rental value. As the rental value of land varied according to its use, one cannot determine a family's income from the enumeration of parcels settled. However, in one of the settlements employing the 'two-pronged' trust, the rental value does appear.[74] Bearing in mind that both the amount of provisions and the rental value of the estates under settlement of the entire body of landed society which employed these trusts varied greatly, this example may be considered to determine whether the provisions for younger sons and daughters which were stipulated in this particular settlement were reasonable given the income generated by the patrimony.

In 1709, Lord Rockingham settled his patrimony upon the marriage of his eldest son, Edward, with Lady Catherine Tufton, daughter of the Earl of Thanet. Estates to the value of £2,000 per annum were settled upon Edward for life, followed by a jointure of £1,300 which was to increase to £1,600 upon the death of the Earl of Faversham.[75] Lord Rockingham covenanted that the entire value of the patrimony exceeded £3,000 per annum. However, he reserved a term of 300 years in trust to raise £15,000 for his own daughters' portions. Moreover, a term was limited for 400 years after the expiration of the life estate in the groom and the jointure estate in the bride to raise a further £15,000 to be appointed amongst the younger sons and daughters produced by the marriage. Thus, over a period of two generations, £30,000 was to be raised out of an estate worth £3,000 per annum.

Calculating the capital value of the estate at 20 years' purchase,[76]

74 Sequence no. 111.
75 The second Earl of Faversham died on 19 April 1709, less than one month after the marriage. Thus the jointure was increased to £1,600 should Edward predecease Lady Catherine. Upon the death of the second Earl of Faversham, an estate of £3,000 descended upon Lord Rockingham's wife Catherine, daughter of the first Earl of Faversham: G.E.C., XI, 58. This might explain Lord Rockingham's generosity, but part of the inheritance may have been expended to provide for his two younger sons.
76 Dr Clay has estimated the price of freehold land during the period 1705–14 to be 20 years' purchase. Clay, 'Freehold land', Table 1. I am assuming th the Rockinghams would be unable to raise these portions by savings. See Habakkuk, 'Marriage settlements', 16.

that is £60,000, one-half of the estate would have to be mortgaged by the time the eldest son produced by the marriage came into possession if he had a brother or sister. One-half of the debt would be contracted upon the death of Lord Rockingham and his wife, and the other half upon the deaths of the bride and groom. Under the settlement, when Edward came into possession of the patrimony, he would have to secure a mortgage to raise £15,000 for his sisters' portions. Merely to meet the interest upon the debt, his net disposable income would be diminished by one-quarter, from £3,000 to £2,250;[77] and upon the succession of his eldest son, one-half of the income from the Rockingham patrimony would be devoted to debt service. What must have been the saving grace for the family was their propensity towards marrying wealthy heiresses. Lady Catherine brought a portion of £13,000 and her son married an heiress as well.[78] Thus the decrease in the income of the patrimony by borrowing was to some extent offset by incoming portions.

To return to the original question, was the landed class able to afford to endow its younger sons and daughters in such a manner, the answer must be a qualified 'yes'; so long as incoming portions balanced outgoing portions, an equilibrium was maintained because the need to mortgage was diminished. It must be stressed, however, that marriage portions were not merely gratuitous payments; the portion was the contribution of the bride's family to her maintenance. As Professor Habakkuk notes, by the late seventeenth century a 'standard ratio' of £1 of jointure for every £10 of portion emerged.[79] Let us consider the 'profit' to the Rockingham inheritance on Lady Catherine Tufton's portion. Assume that the £13,000 was invested in land in 1709; the return on the investment would be £520 per annum.[80] Lady Catherine died in 1734, twenty-five years after marriage. During the period, £13,000 of income was generated by her portion; yet she survived her husband by twelve years, and her jointure of £1,600 per annum cost

77 The standard rate of interest on mortgages during the period was 5%. Clay, 'Marriage, inheritance', 508.
78 K.A.O. U791 T284. Katherine Furnese, sister and heir of Sir Henry Furnese, Baronet (sequence no. 141). Unfortunately the settlement does not recite the extent of the Furnese inheritance, but G.E.C. (XI, 58) estimated the fortune at £200,000.
79 Habakkuk, 'Marriage settlements', 20–1.
80 Dr Clay suggests 4% as an accurate return given repairs, administration and taxes: 'Marriage, inheritance', 508.

the Rockingham inheritance £19,000. It would take an additional eleven years before the return upon the £13,000 portion equalled the charge for her jointure. Admittedly, portions could be windfalls, but only where the widows did not survive their husbands for long periods. Yet amongst the Northamptonshire peerage, Lady Catherine's longevity was 'typical'. During the period 1601–1740, the mean number of years which wives survived their husbands was 11.7. Amongst the Kentish peerage, it was 16.3.[81] This statistic, as well as another vital point, must be considered when assessing the importance of marriage in the 'rise of great estates': those families which could command brides with the largest portions were also inclined to endow their own daughters and younger sons most handsomely.

Having illustrated the transformation in the mechanical form which provisions for younger sons and daughters assumed, as well as its economic ramifications, the suggestion of economic historians that daughters were in practice more generously endowed than their brothers may be considered.[82] During the period 1660–1740, twenty-six marriage settlements contain provisions for younger sons and daughters by inserting a limitation of a term before the remainder to the eldest son. In thirteen of these settlements (50%), the method of distribution was specified; younger sons and daughters were to share the sum *equally*.[83] Under the provisions of the other thirteen settlements (50%), the father was empowered to appoint the sum as he pleased; in default of appointment, all the surviving younger sons and daughters were again to take *equal shares*.[84] With regard to discretionary powers of appointment during the period, ten of the fifteen included in my data set allowed the father to favour a particular child.[85] But in no marriage settlement included in my data set were the daughters *directed* to receive a larger share of the allotted sum.

Thus if the daughters were indeed more generously endowed than their brothers, it was on an *ad hoc* basis. That equal distribution amongst younger sons and daughters was mandated in

---

81 Data derived from *G.E.C.*
82 Habakkuk, 'Daniel Finch, 2nd Earl of Nottingham', 157; Mingay, *English landed society*, 29.
83 Sequence nos. 75, 76, 95, 101, 105, 114, 121, 130, 131, 140, 274, 275, 279.
84 Sequence nos. 108, 111, 122, 129, 135, 136, 139, 140, 268, 272, 273, 277, 280.
85 Sequence nos. 67, 82, 86, 90, 95, 103, 116, 126, 127, 129, 241, 250, 262, 269, 271;
   of these sequence nos. 86, 90, 116, 250, 262, 271 directed equal distribution.

the majority of trusts, and in default of appointment, tends to indicate that it was the conscious policy of most settlors; had they believed that it was necessary to endow their daughters or grand-daughters more generously than their younger sons, then they certainly could have directed the distribution in their favour. What is clear, however, is that settlors were far more concerned with their daughters and granddaughters than with their collateral heirs. Considerable increases in portions were often mandated by the second term.[86]

To conclude, it would appear that the period 1601–1740 witnessed a dramatic transformation in the means by which landowners provided for their daughters and younger sons. In the sixty years which preceded the advent of the strict settlement, the will rather than the marriage settlement served as the vehicle for directing portions. Where portions were directed by marriage settlement, they were either discretionary or conditional upon the failure of the marriage to produce a surviving male child. With the adoption of the strict settlement, the trust became the most common mechanism to raise portions. Yet as the marriage settlements in my data set illustrate, it was not until the turn of the eighteenth century that trusts providing for younger sons and daughters were implemented which took effect regardless of whether the marriage produced a male heir. Thus it would appear that Blackstone's suggestion that the desire to fix provisions for prospective younger sons and daughters was not the paramount factor which led conveyancers to develop the strict settlement is incorrect. Rather, it was not until the settlement came into widespread use that its potential for securing portions was realized.

Finally, this enquiry into the patterns of provision during the period 1601–1740 has established that the method eventually adopted by many great landowners was rather costly. Unlike the form initially adopted in strict settlements, which directed portions only upon collateral inheritances, the emerging form provided for portions in each generation, often compelling the eldest son to

---

86 For example, Lord Teynham directed a maximum of £8,000 (sequence no. 105); the Earl of Rockingham allowed £15,000 with an additional £16,000 if no male was produced by the marriage (sequence no. 111); Viscount St John allowed £20,000, with an additional £10,000 if no son was produced (sequence no. 131); and the Earl of Rockingham apportioned £24,000, with an additional £15,000 if no son was produced (sequence no. 141).

resort to mortgaging. But it was only after a number of successions, and thus around the mid-eighteenth century that the debt service would have become unbearable.

To some extent the strict settlement was the solution to the controversy over primogeniture. The adoption by many families of a secure method of providing portions for younger sons mitigated the harshness of the law of descent. No longer was the younger son left with, as Thomas Wilson complained, 'that which the cat left on the malt heap'; and as Professor Habakkuk has noted, the provision of a capital sum enabled the younger son to establish himself in trade or the professions. Whether the transformation which we have observed should be attributed to trends in the development of familial relationships, such as the rise of the 'closed domesticated nuclear family', 'affective individualism', or the 'egalitarian family', is, of course, a matter for speculation.[87] But it is family muniments such as we have chosen to exploit that will provide a more satisfying answer than the complaints, apologies or ruminations of contemporaries. The present investigation into patterns of provisions for 'excess children' demonstrates that in the eighteenth century there was a shift towards greater equality in the distribution of family wealth.

But in the end this new-found 'social consciousness' had to be paid for. The elaborate system of trusts implemented in many settlements after the turn of the century generally required the eldest son to mortgage the patrimony. And, as the Rockingham example attests, this process made substantial inroads upon the disposable income of the tenant in possession. To some extent, and obviously to varying degrees depending upon the particular family's success in the 'marriage market', incoming portions might compensate for outgoing provisions. Once again, however, it must be recognized that a family's economic fortune was often at the mercy of demography; and when economic historians consider the importance of marriage portions in the 'rise of great estates', they must realize that large portions from brides were not necessarily windfalls. Often these staggering sums merely preserved the status quo.

87 The first two terms are those of Lawrence Stone in *The family, sex and marriage in England 1500–1800* (London, 1977), chapter 7; the latter is that of R. Trumbach, *The rise of the egalitarian family: aristocratic kinship and domestic relations in eighteenth century England* (London, 1978), Introduction.

CONCLUSION

The business of the historian is to illuminate and understand change over time. To accomplish the former is relatively straightforward assuming the appropriate evidence survives; to attempt the latter is always dangerous and sometimes even reckless. The focus of this study has been upon illumination: to chart the evolution in the legal form and financial arrangements embodied in marriage settlements over two centuries. In many respects the documents speak for themselves. We know that landed society, assisted by the legal profession, came to fix the transmission of the patrimony and the distribution of familial wealth, that is to produce what modern lawyers would call an 'estate plan', at a particular time: the marriage of the male heir.

Why they did so is less clear. The documents themselves are silent upon the matter, and the explanations of both contemporaries and historians are, when scrutinized, not altogether satisfying. Certain hypotheses which have been formulated by historians of the family concerning the emotional content of family relationships, if they could be substantiated by further research, may well explain this transformation in estate settlement.

For it is indeed inviting to attribute the changes discussed above to the development of 'the closed domesticated nuclear family' and the growth of 'affective individualism'. The 'estate plan' which landed society adopted in the late seventeenth and early eighteenth centuries can be seen to have limited the patriarchal capacity of fathers by circumscribing their powers over disinheritance. The notion that the wealth of the family should be more equitably distributed between the male heir and 'excess children' suggests a desire to insure that one's children or grandchildren would avoid downward social mobility, or at least that the decision to allow it would not rest with one man. Moreover, the institution of pin money does evince a stronger recognition of the wife's right to separate property, though the Chancery's determination to protect her interests was apparent long before this family type is said to have been developed.[1] Finally, the tendency to provide that one's estate should be divided amongst surviving daughters, rather than descend to a collateral male heir, a pattern of disposition which became increasingly common in the course of the late seventeenth century, seems to indicate that the notion of patrilineal descent, and perhaps of kinship itself, was on the wane.

But it would be unwise for historians who wish to understand the interplay between legal practice and society to look no further for contributing factors. The period under study was also one of economic change. Although the general movement of rents and prices is said to have been unfavourable, the improving landowner may well have had more wealth at his disposal. Its more even distribution, and in particular the endowment of 'excess children', might be effected even without a fundamental change in the nature of the family.

But perhaps more significantly, the hundred years after the civil war were ones of serious demographic difficulties in many landed families. The production of fewer children who survived to the age of majority would have an effect upon the proportion of family resources which they required. Generosity and the securing of it becomes more understandable. Moreover, the dwindling production of males would likely demand a different strategy of heirship. Maintaining younger sons and daughters who did survive so that they may be called upon should the presumptive heir die might seem prudent to a peer or squire aware of such things as generation replacement rates.

While recognizing the fit between the patterns of settlement uncovered by this study and the proffered trend in familial relationships, these other considerations make it appropriate for historians to ruminate further upon the causes of change.[2] Few elites, even those so consumed with affect as the eighteenth-century English landed class are said to have been, willingly commit economic suicide. To some degree, then, the financial relationships within the family must have been governed by supply and demand factors. It is for economic, social and legal historians to take notice of the trends illuminated here to strike a balance amongst competing concerns in order to understand more precisely why the period witnessed such a dramatic and interesting alteration in 'estate planning' techniques.

1 Sequence nos. 79, 81, 103, 109, 131, 263, 275.
2 I hope to discuss these issues more fully elsewhere.

BIBLIOGRAPHY

PRIMARY SOURCES

1. Manuscripts

Bradford Papers, Weston Park: Class 5/7
British Library: Hardwicke MSS 85, 35863, 1877; Harleian MS 2053;
    Hargrave MSS 55-8; Lansdowne MS 216; Additional MSS 25240,
    29871, 36077
Cambridge University Library: MS Dd. ii. 46, Ee. i. 6, Ee. iv. 1, Gg. ii. 31;
    Additional MS 6235
Inner Temple Library: Barrington MSS 27, 80
Kent Archives Office: U120 T125; U120 T200/10, 14, 16; U455 T280/1, 2;
    U455 T282; U791 T284; U1063 T45; Sequence nos. 1-146 (below,
    pp. 128-31)
Leicestershire Record Office: Barker MSS DE 730/1; DE 730/4-5; Conant
    MS DG 11/960; Palmer MSS 623-7, 630
Northamptonshire Record Office: M(TM) 575; Finch MSS, Correspon-
    dence no. 515; Sequence nos. 201-80 (below, pp. 132-3)
Public Record Office: Prerogative Court of Canterbury: PROB 11/114,
    PROB 11/160, PROB 11/333
State Papers: Committee for Compounding, G.3, G.192

2. Printed sources

Foster, J., ed. *The register of admissions to Gray's Inn* (London, 1889)
Historical Manuscripts Commission *Report on the manuscripts of the late
    Allan George Finch* (London, 1922)
Publications of the Surtees Society, vol. LXXVII (1883)
Robertson, A. J. *Anglo-Saxon charters* (Cambridge, 1939)
Students admitted to the Inner Temple, 1547-1660 (London, 1877)

3. Printed books

Bacon, F. *Works of Lord Bacon*, ed. J. Spedding (London, 1857)
Blackstone, W. *Commentaries on the Laws of England*, 4th edn (London,
    1770)
Bracton on the laws and customs of England, ed. G. E. Woodbine, trans. S. E.
    Thorne (4 vols., Cambridge, Mass., 1968-)
Bridgeman's Reports, ed. S. Bannister (London, 1823)
Coke, E. *The first part of the institutes of the laws of England, or a commentary
    on Littleton*, 18th edn, ed. F. Hargrave and C. Butler (London, 1823)
Cook, J. *Monarchy no creature of God's making* (Waterford, 1651)
Delamer, H. *The works of the Right Honourable Henry late Lord Delamer*
    (London, 1694)

Fearne, C. *An essay on the learning of contingent remainders*, 7th edn (London, 1820)

Finch, H. *Lord Nottingham's Chancery cases*, ed. D. E. C. Yale (Selden Society, London, 1957)

Lord Nottingham's manual of Chancery practice and prolegomena of Chancery and Equity, ed. D. E. C. Yale (Cambridge, 1965)

Glanvill *The treatise on the laws and customs of the realm of England commonly called Glanvill*, ed. G. D. G. Hall (London, 1965)

Hale, M. *A treatise concerning the enrollment of deeds* (London, 1694)

The history of the common law of England, ed. Charles M. Gray (Chicago, 1971)

Hasted, E. *The history and topographical survey of the county of Kent* (Canterbury, 1778–99)

Lambarde, W. *A perambulation of Kent* (London, 1596)

The lawes resolution of women's rights (London, 1632)

Littleton, T. *Littleton's tenures in English*, ed. E. Wambaugh (Washington, 1903)

March, J. *Amicus republicae: the Commonwealth's friend* (Lonodn, 1651)

Noy, W. *The complete lawyer or a treatise concerning tenures* (London, 1651)

Powell, T. *The attorney's academy* (London, 1623)

St German's Doctor and student, ed. T. F. T. Plucknett and J. Barton (Selden Society, London, 1974)

Sheppard, W. *An epitome of all the common and statute laws of the nation* (London, 1656)

England's balme (London, 1657)

A grand abridgement of the common and statute law of England (3 vols., London, 1675)

Somers, John *A collection of scarce and valuable tracts*, 2nd edn (13 vols., London, 1809–15)

Spelman's reports, ed. J. H. Baker (2 vols., Selden Society, London: vol 93, 1977; vol. 94, 1978)

Swinburne, H. *A brief treatise of testaments and last wills* (London, 1635)

The use of the law (London, 1629)

Viner, C. *A general abridgement of law and equity*, 2nd edn (24 vols., London, 1797)

Wilson, T. *The state of England, Anno Dom. 1600* Camden Miscellany, xvi (1936)

4. Conveyancing books

Billinghurst, G. *Arcania clericalia: or the mysteries of clerkship explained* (London, 1674)

Bridgeman's conveyances, 2nd edn (London, 1690)

Compleat conveyancer; A collection of presidents for conveyances (London, 1701)

Complete clark, containing the best forms of all sorts of precedents for conveyances and assurances (London, 1664)

Conveyancer's assistant and director: being a treatise containing tables to all sorts of conveyances (London, 1702)

Exact book of most approved precedents (London, 1663)
Exact clark and scrivener: a compendium of all manner of precedents now in use (London, 1659)
Fidell, T. *A perfect guide for the studious young lawyer* (London, 1654)
Herne, J. *The modern assurancer: or the clerk's directory* (London, 1658)
Hutton, R. *The young clerk's guide, or an exact collection of choice English precedents* (London, 1670)
Madox, T. *Formulare Anglicanum* (London, 1702)
The modern conveyancer (London, 1695)
The perfect conveyancer: or several select and choice presidents (London, 1655)
Phayer, T. *A newe boke of presidents in manner of a register* (London, 1543)
Sheppard, W. *The touchstone of common assurances* (London, 1651)
The president of presidents: or one General president for common assurances by deeds (London, 1655)
West, W. *Symbolaeographia* (London, 1590)

SECONDARY SOURCES

1. Printed books and articles

Aydelotte, W. O. *Quantification in history* (Reading, Mass., 1971)
Barton, J. L. 'Future interests and royal revenues in the sixteenth century', in *On the laws and customs of England: essays in honor of Samuel E. Thorne*, ed. M. S. Arnold, T. A. Green, S. A. Scully and S. D. White (Chapel Hill, North Carolina, 1981)
Bean, J. M. W. *The decline of English feudalism 1250–1540* (Manchester, 1968)
The estates of the Percy family 1416–1537 (Cambridge, 1958)
Beckett, J. V. 'English landownership in the later seventeenth and eighteenth century: the debate and the problems', *Econ. Hist. Rev.*, 2nd ser. XXX (1977)
Bonfield, L. 'Marriage settlements and the "rise of great estates": the demographic aspect', *Econ. Hist. Rev.*, 2nd ser. XXXII (1979)
'Marriage settlements and the "rise of great estates": a rejoinder', *Econ. Hist. Rev.*, 2nd ser. XXXIII (1980)
'Marriage settlements 1660–1740; the adoption of the strict settlement in Kent and Northamptonshire', in *Marriage and society*, ed. R. B. Outhwaite (London, 1981)
Bridgeman, R. O. and Bridgeman, C. O. 'The sequestration papers of Sir Orlando Bridgeman', *Transactions of the Shropshire Archaeological Society*, 3rd ser. II (1902)
Cannadine, D. 'Aristocratic indebtedness in the nineteenth century: the case re-opened', *Econ. Hist. Rev.*, 2nd ser. XXX (1977)
Chalklin, C. W. *Seventeenth century Kent* (London, 1965)
Challis, H. W. *Law of real property*, 3rd edn (London, 1911)
Clark, P. *English provincial society from the reformation to the revolution* (Sussex, 1977)
'The price of freehold land in the later seventeenth and eighteenth century', *Econ. Hist Rev.*, 2nd ser. XXXVII (1974)

Clay, C. 'Marriage, inheritance and the rise of large estates in England 1660–1815', *Econ. Hist. Rev.*, 2nd ser. XXI (1968)

Coleman, D. C. *Sir John Banks: baronet and businessman* (Oxford, 1963)

Cooper, J. P. 'The social distribution of land and men in England 1436–1700', *Econ. Hist. Rev.*, 2nd ser. XX (1967)

'Patterns of inheritance and settlement by great landowners from the fifteenth to the eighteenth centuries', in *Family and inheritance*, ed. J. Goody, J. Thirsk and E. P. Thompson (Cambridge, 1976)

Cotterell, M. 'Interregnum law reform: the Hale Commission of 1652', *E.H.R.*, LXXXIII (1968)

Coward, B. 'Disputed inheritances: some problems of the nobility in the sixteenth and early seventeenth century', *B.I.H.R.*, XLIV (1971)

Elton, G. R. 'Parliamentary drafts, 1529–1540', *B.I.H.R.*, XXV (1952)

English, B., and Saville, J. 'Family settlement and the "rise of great estates"', *Econ. Hist. Rev.*, 2nd ser. XXXIII (1980)

Everitt, A. M. 'Social mobility in early modern England', *Past and Present*, XXX (1966)

The community of Kent and the great rebellion (Leicester, 1973)

Finch, M. E. *Five Northamptonshire families* (Northamptonshire Record Society, Oxford, 1956)

Floud, R. *An introduction to quantitative methods for historians* (London, 1973)

Gray, J. C. *The rule against perpetuities* (Boston, Mass., 1886)

Habakkuk, H. J. 'English landownership 1680–1740', *Econ. Hist. Rev.*, X (1940)

'Marriage settlements in the eighteenth century', *T.R.H.S.*, 4th ser. XXXII (1950)

'The long term rate of interest and the price of freehold land in the seventeenth century', *Econ. Hist Rev.*, 2nd ser. X (1952)

'Social attitudes and attributes', in *The European nobility in the eighteenth century*, ed. A. Goodwin (London, 1953)

'Daniel Finch, 2nd Earl of Nottingham: his house and estate', in *Studies in social history*, ed. J. H. Plumb (London, 1955)

'The English land market in the eighteenth century', in *Britain and the Netherlands*, ed. J. S. Bromley and E. H. Krossman (London, 1960)

'La disparation du paysan anglais', *Annales*, XX (1965)

'Economic functions of English landowners in the seventeenth and eighteenth century', in *Essays in Agrarian History*, ed. W. E. Minchinton (London, 1968)

Haskins, G. L. 'Extending the grasp of the dead hand: reflections on the origins of the rule against perpetuities', *University of Pennsylvania Law Review*, CXXV (1977)

Holderness, B. A. 'The English land market in the eighteenth century: the case of Lincolnshire', *Econ. Hist. Rev.*, 2nd ser. XXVII (1974)

Holdsworth, W. *A history of English law* (16 vols., London, 1922–66)

Hollingsworth, T. H. 'The demography of the British peerage', Supplement to *Population Studies*, XVIII (1964)

'Mortality in the British peerage families', *Population*, XXXII (1977)

Ives, E. W. 'The genesis of the Statute of Uses', *E.H.R.*, LXXXII (1967)

Kelch, R. A. *Newcastle: A duke without money* (London, 1974)

Laslett, T. P. R. 'The gentry of Kent in 1640', *Cambridge Historical Journal*, X (1949)

McFarlane, K. B. *The nobility of later medieval England* (Oxford, 1973)

Milsom, S. F. C. *Historical foundations of the common law*, 2nd edn (London, 1981)

Mingay, G. E. *English landed society in the eighteenth century* (London, 1963)

Parker, R. A. C. *Coke of Norfolk: a financial and agricultural study 1702–1842* (Oxford, 1975)

Plucknett, T. F. T. *Concise history of the common law*, 4th edn (London, 1947)

Pollock, F. *The land laws*, 2nd edn (London, 1887)

Pollock, F., and Maitland, F. W. *The history of English law before the time of Edward I*, 2nd edn (Cambridge, 1968)

Robinson, T. *The common law of Kent: or the customs of gavelkind* (London, 1788)

Schlesinger, A. Jr. 'The humanist looks at empirical social research', *American Sociological Review*, 27 (1962)

Simpson, A. W. B. *An introduction to the history of the land law* (Oxford, 1961)

Stone, L. *The crisis of the aristocracy, 1558–1641* (Oxford, 1965)

The family, sex and marriage in England 1500–1800 (London, 1977)

Sweet, C. 'Contingent remainders and other possibilities', *Yale Law Journal*, XXVII (1917)

'Double possibilities', *Law Quarterly Review*, XXX (1914)

Thirsk, J. 'The European debate on customs of inheritance, 1500–1700', in *Family and inheritance*, ed. J. Goody, J. Thirsk, and E. P. Thompson (Cambridge, 1976)

Thompson, F. M. L. 'The social distribution of landed property in England since the sixteenth century', *Econ. Hist. Rev.*, 2nd ser. XIX (1966)

'Landownership and economic growth in England in the eighteenth century', in *Agrarian change and economic development*, ed. E. J. Jones and S. L. Woolf (London, 1970)

Trumbach, R. *The rise of the egalitarian family aristocratic kinship and domestic relations in eighteenth century England* (London, 1978)

Williams, J. 'On the origins of the present mode of family settlements of landed property', *Papers read before the Juridical Society*, I (1855–8)

Wrigley, E. A. 'Fertility strategy for the individual and the group', in *Historical studies of changing fertility*, ed. C. Tilly (Princeton, 1978)

Yale, D. E. C. 'The revival of equitable estates in the seventeenth century: an explanation by Lord Nottingham', *Cambridge Law Journal* (1957)

Young, E. 'The Anglo-Saxon family law', in *Essays in Anglo-Saxon law* (Boston, Mass., 1905)

2. Unpublished theses

Bonfield, L. 'Marriage settlements 1601–1740: the development and adoption of the strict settlement' (Unpublished University of Cambridge Ph.D. thesis, 1978)

Cioni, M. L. 'Women and law in Elizabethan England with particular reference to the Court of Chancery' (University of Cambridge Ph.D. thesis, 1974)

Clay, C. 'Two families and their estates: the Grimstones and the Cowpers from c.1650–c.1815' (University of Cambridge Ph.D. thesis, 1966)

Coleman, D. C. 'The economy of Kent under the later Stuarts' (Unpublished University of London Ph.D. thesis, 1951)

Everitt, A. M. 'Kent and its gentry, 1640–60, a political study' (Unpublished University of London Ph.D. thesis, 1957)

KEY RELATING SEQUENCE NUMBERS TO ARCHIVE REFERENCES

Kent Archives Office

SEQUENCE NUMBER	K.A.O. REFERENCE	DATE
1	U455 T280	1602
2	U908 T245	1602
3	U791 T247	1603
4	U6 T17	1605
5	U269 T69/1	1606
6	U522 T128/2	1606
7	U813 T33/4	1606
8	U1015 T1/B6	1607
9	U214 T507	1608
10	U1115 T123	1610
11	U771 T162	1611
12	U908 T255/1	1614
13	U1006 T61	1615
14	U1875 T1	1616
15	U120 T171	1618
16	U275 T1	1619
17	U120 T172	1620
18	U962 T26	1621
19	U737 T3/1	1624
20	U275 T2	1624
21	U1118 T7/2	1626
22	U145 T87/1	1627
23a and b	U455 T281	1629
24	U593 T1	1631
25	U813 T44/1	1632

SEQUENCE NUMBER	K.A.O. REFERENCE	DATE
26	U269 T79/1	1633
27	U1015 T1/B	1633
28	U1936 T1/4	1636
29	U1255 T19	1636
30	U1255 T82	1636
31a	U908 T257/3	1636
31b	U908 T257/4	1636
32	U565 T1	1637
33	U33 E1	1639
34	U229 T301	1640
35	U55 T653	1642
36	U908 T258	1644
37	U477 T68/1	1649
38	U1063 T68	1649
39	U24 T284	1650
40	U1246 T51	1651
41	U548 T33	1652
42	U97 T46	1653
43	U38 T38	1656
44	U725 T163	1657
45a and b	U1007 E123	1659
46	U36 T795	1660
47	U106 T1/12	1660
48	U830 T6	1660
49	U38 T39	1661
50	U679 T15/1	1661
51	U145 T2	1662
52	U806 T104	1662
53	U1255 T83	1662
54	U193 E3	1664
55	U806 T145	1664
56	U455 T282	1664
57	U1255 T84	1665
58	U82 T135	1667
59a and b	U908 T264	1666
60	U229 T317	1669
61	U282 F6	1671
62	U312 T18	1671
63	U565 T211	1672
64	U438 T137	1673
65	U962 T25	1674

SEQUENCE NUMBER	K.A.O. REFERENCE	DATE
66	U1449 T14	1674
67	U806 T1/B6	1675
68	U967 T12/B2	1676
69	U145 T89/3–4	1677
70	U774 T775	1678
71	U409 T38	1680
72	U1584 T1	1680
73	U1255 T87	1681
74	U771 T166	1681
75	U120 T173	1682
76	U806 T80/B5	1682
77	U36 T533	1682
78	U1255 T89	1682
79	U1592 E11	1683
80	U38 T42	1684
81	U269 T6975	1685
82	U455 T283	1686
83	U771 T169	1687
84	U88 T61	1688
85	U229 T28	1688
86	U120 T181	1688
87	U1854 T1/B1	1689
88	U1015 T25	1689
89	U1015 T24	1689
90	U120 T182	1690
91	U1255 T90	1690
92	U120 T182	1690
93	U214 T432	1694
94	U962 T111	1694
95	U36 T447	1698
96	U576 T4/2	1699
97	U1666 T5	1699
98	U1255 T92	1699
99	U55 T648	1701
100	U49 T48/1A	1701
101	U967 T13	1701
102	U1006 T5B/B2	1701
103	U1015 T17/3	1703
104	U480 T154	1703
105	U498 T11	1704
106	U908 T270	1704

SEQUENCE NUMBER	K.A.O. REFERENCE	DATE
107	U908 T269	1704
108	U120 T175	1706
109	U813 T44/4	1707
110	U771 T172	1707
111	U791 T248	1708
112	U908 T271	1708
113	U771 T173	1708
114	U1236 T26	1709
115	U962 T25	1709
116	U774 T713	1709
117	U522 T127/7	1716
118	U725 T156	1717
119	U1015 T26	1717
120a and b	U1015 T27/1	1718
121	U36 T796	1718
122	U1007 E134	1719
123	U38 T45	1720
124	U806 T106	1722
125	U82 T396	1722
126	U1255 T94	1723
127	U309 T37	1724
128	U806 T86	1725
129	U36 T474	1726
130	U1175 T65	1729
131	U36 T385	1729
132	U480 T158	1729
133	U145 T90/3	1729
134	U38 T43	1730
135	U145 T90/4	1730
136	U1045 T12A	1730
137	U145 T90/5	1731
138	U145 T89/5	1732
139	U1836 T1	1734
140	U82 T135	1736
141	U471 T128	1736
142	U678 T28/1	1736
143	U1352 T1	1737
144	U769 T31	1737
145	U179 T1	1738
146	U855 T212	1740

Northamptonshire Record Office

SEQUENCE NUMBER	N.R.O. REFERENCE	DATE
201	D(CA) 599	1601
202	SJ 1	1602
203	I(L) 2117	1607
204	T(S) Box 3 Bdl 5/8	1610
205	Fitzwilliam MSS 2127	1610
206	H(K) 9	1610
207	ZA 3850	1612
208	O(K) 125	1613
209	B(O) Box 320/4–54	1617
210	SS 454a (A.1.4)	1621
211	SS454a/1	1621
212	W(C) 87	1622
213	SJ 22	1623
214	H(BL) 1144	1626
215	B(D) 449	1627
216	E(B) 732	1627
217	ZA 7703	1631
218	H(BL) 668	1632
219	D(CA) 517	1632
220	Brudenell MSS K.xi.12	1633
221	(C) 3067	1633
222	B(O) Box 320/4	1633
223	Fitzwilliam MSS 2130	1633
224	I(L) 2381	1634
225	S(G) 437	1634
226	Westmorland MSS Box 1, Parcel X, No. 7	1636
227	Westmorland MSS Box 1, Parcel X, No. 8	1638
228	Brudenell MSS K.vii.2	1641
229	Th 1678	1641
230	YZ 1545	1642
231	TB 247/1	1646
232	TB 247/2	1646
233	S(G) 680	1648
234	W(C) 60	1650
235	Powys MSS Group 2 (4981)	1652
236	I(L) 468	1653
237	ASL 910	1655
238	SJ 65	1656
239	H(K) 9	1657
240	Th 2579	1660

SEQUENCE NUMBER	N.R.O. REFERENCE	DATE
241	E(B) 207	1664
242	Westmorland MSS Box 1, Parcel X, No. 10	1665
243	Brudenell MSS K.xiii.2	1668
244	C(A) Box 105	1669
245	Westmorland MSS Box 1, Parcel X, No. 11	1671
246	Fermor MSS Box H Bdl III/1	1671
247	E(B) 214/1	1673
248	E(B) 214/2	1674
249	Powys MSS Group 3 (4983)	1674
250	FH 3101	1675
251	BH(K) 216	1677
252	TB 265/1	1677
253	TB 265/2	1677
254	YZ 7500	1681
255	YO 980	1682
256	I(L) 755	1683
257	Fermor MSS Box H Bdl III/2	1683
258	YZ 7695	1689
259	Fermor MSS Box H Bdl III/3	1691
260	TB 318	1694
261	B(D) 450	1696
262	C(A) 6445	1698
263	C(A) 60	1699
264	GI 187	1699
265	TB 271/2	1701
266	TB 271	1701
267	GI 189	1704
268	BH(K) 217	1706
269	Brudenell MSS G.i.12	1708
270	D(CA) 524	1710
271	GI 190	1711
272	I(L) 1249A	1722
273	Botfield MSS Bdl 12	1723
274	SJ 151	1725
275	I(L) 1412	1725
276	YZ 1050	1726
277	C(A) 62	1726
278	M(W) 217	1728
279	HT(A) 37	1731
280	L(T) 381	1732

INDEX

annuities, 105, 111

Bacon, Sir Francis, 11–12, 16, 23–4
Billinghurst, George, 63–4
Blackstone, Sir William, xiv, 58, 102, 109
Bridgeman, Sir Orlando, 58, 60–6, 69–71

cases, law and equity
  Archer's Case, 33–4, 59
  Basset v. *Clapham*, 79
  Brent's Case, 36
  Childe v. *Baille*, 38–9
  Cholmley's Case, 59, 71, 75–6
  Chudleigh's Case, 11–12, 14, 34, 36, 44, 59
  Colethirst v. *Bejushin*, 25, 28–30, 47
  Corbet's Case, 41–2, 44
  Davies v. *Weld*, 77
  Dormer v. *Parkhurst*, 71, 74–7, 79, 81
  Duke of Norfolk's Case, 39, 77
  Duncomb v. *Duncomb*, 71–4, 76–8
  Elie v. *Osborne*, 79–80
  Garth v. *Cotton*, 58
  Lampet's Case, 37–8
  Lewis Bowles's Case, 33–4, 51, 72–3
  Lovelace v. *Lovelace*, 43
  Manning's Case, 37–9
  Mansell v. *Mansell*, 80
  Mary Portington's Case, 41–2, 44, 46
  Pells v. *Brown*, 38–9
  Platt v. *Spugg*, 78
  Pye v. *George*, 78
  Rector of Chedington's Case, 35
  Rudhall v. *Milwards*, 40
  Scholastica's Case, 40–2, 46
  Shelley's Case, 25, 32–3, 51
  Tipping v. *Piggot*, 79
  Wild's Case, 25, 30–1
  Wiseman's Case, 40

Chancery, court of, 37, 43, 57–8, 71–81
Coke, Sir Edward, 3–5, 16–17, 22–3, 35, 42, 59–60, 76
common recovery, 13, 38, 74
contingent remainders, 12, 24–35, 43, 46–54, 55–60, 73–81
conveyancing manuals, 9, 44, 63–6, 82, 86
Cook, John, 20
copyhold, 70

De donis, 17
dower, 1–10

entail, 8–9, 13, 16–24, 40–2, 46–54, 55–60
executory interests, 24, 35–46

Fearne, Charles, 56–7

gavelkind, xvii

Hale, Matthew, 15, 23
Hale Commission, 21
Hardwicke, Lord Chancellor (Phillip Yorke), 58–60, 72, 76

jointure, 2–10, 47–54, 84, 94, 98–100, 107

Kent, xvi–xvii, 47–52, 64, 86, 89–91, 99, 100, 113

landownership patterns, 82, 90, 92–102, 116–18
legal profession, 65–6, 82–3, 92

morgengifu, 1
mortgages, 50, 95, 99, 103, 115

Northamptonshire, xvii, 46–52, 64, 86, 90–1, 107, 114

Noy, William, 19

Palmer, Sir Geoffrey, 58, 66–70
perpetuities, 8, 14–15, 22–4, 36–7,
    39–46, 57
Pollexfen, Sir Henry, 77
portions, 70, 84, 94–5, 98–100, 102–20
'possibilities', 34–5
powers of appointment, 105–7, 112–14
primogeniture, 15, 20

St German, Christopher, 17–18
seisin, 27–32
settlement, 'life estate-entail', 8–9,
    47–54
settlement, strict, 8, 55–81, 82–92,
    94–6, 101–4, 109–15, 119
Sheppard, William, 19–20, 43, 52, 72

Tenures, Statute of, 71
terms of years, 27, 37, 70, 74–6
trust to preserve contingent
    remainders, 31, 53–4, 55, 81, 101,
    110
trust to raise portions, 105, 108,
    109–20

uses, 1–2, 14, 36–45, 70
Uses, Statute of, 2–3, 6–10, 11–12, 14,
    24, 26, 36–8, 70

Ventris, Sir Peyton, 86–7
Viner, Charles, 73, 75–6

wills, 104–6
Wills, Statute of, 24

CAMBRIDGE STUDIES IN ENGLISH LEGAL HISTORY

The Law of Treason in England
in the Later Middle Ages
J. G. BELLAMY

The Equity Side of the Exchequer
W. H. BRYSON

The High Court of Delegates
G. I. O. DUNCAN

Marriage Litigation in Medieval England
R. H. HELMHOLZ

The Ancient State, Authoritie, and
Proceedings of the Court of Requests
by Sir Julius Caesar
EDITED BY L. M. HILL

Law and Politics in Jacobean England:
The Tracts of Lord Chancellor Ellesmere
LOUIS A. KNAFLA

The Legal Framework of English Feudalism
S. F. C. MILSOM

The Judicial Committee of the Privy Council
1833–1876
P. A. HOWELL

The Common Lawyers of Pre-Reformation England
Thomas Kebell: A Case Study
E. W. IVES